Everything

KATHLEEN CHADA
A MEMOIR

umbrella
PUBLISHING

PUBLISHED BY UMBRELLA PUBLISHING
1 WOODVILLE GREEN
LUCAN
CO. DUBLIN
IRELAND

A CIP record for this book is available from the British Library

ISBN 9781910827642

Cover design and formatting: jessica@viitaladesign.com
Back cover photograph: Dylan Vaughan

♥

DEDICATION

To Eoghan and Ruairi, and everyone who
has tragically lost a child

Foreword

SOME YEARS ago, I talked about what the word 'Choice' means to me and how it has allowed me to embrace the possible. And even the impossible at times. The word choice itself is incredibly powerful. It gives control where there might be none. It gives me control over my own life and how I choose to live it.

On July 29, 2013, my entire life was taken away, leaving me with just the ability to take a breath. My husband and the father of my two sons made a choice to take their lives. And in doing so he took away all choice from both Eoghan and Ruairi and me. That day he took their lives and left me alone. I consider that I lost everything that made me that day. I was no longer a wife and mother, even though I still felt I was.

I lost my confidence in everything and in everyone around me. I lost my trust even of those close to me. I lost my ability to make my own decisions, right down to the ability to choose between a cup of tea and a cup of coffee.

I have always considered myself to be a strong woman. And up until that day I was; I'd never had reason to question that. But after I lost Eoghan and Ruairi, I questioned everything.

However, thankfully, with the help of amazing family and friends, and with brilliant professional care, I chose to live. In many ways, that choice has defined my journey to the person I am today.

I have chosen to live and it is up to me to make that life meaningful. It is so very different to the life I had and will forever long for. But the realisation that I did have a choice and that I had chosen to live, gave me back some sense of control over my life and how I should live it.

The most important choice that I now make every day is to be the voices of my sons. I believe Eoghan and Ruairi were put on this earth to do great things, so now it is my job to be their voice and make sure it is heard. I believe their message is one of love and care. They had an incredibly strong sense of fairness with each other. And this allowed a respect for each other and the choices each made.

I am incredibly proud of my boys for the boys they were, the men they would have become and the angels I know they are today… looking down and watching over me and over all those they love. They continue to inspire me and so many of our family and friends, to live and appreciate our lives more every day. They are and always will be my pride and joy, my greatest achievement. I am so lucky to be their mam and I will hold my lifetime of our memories inside me forever.

I made the choice to write this book for my boys.

The lives they lived, and how the loss of their lives is now helping other families, and will help families who will meet with awful tragedy into the future, led me to make the decision to have Eoghan and Ruairi's story published.

I want to thank everyone who helped Eoghan and Ruairi live their beautiful lives. And, I want to thank everyone who helped me survive their deaths. There are so many people, and too many to mention by name, but thank you all. Especially, my love and thanks forever to the people of my home village, Ballinkillen.

This is a book which, I hope, will save lives.

Kathleen Chada
May 2023

'It's not that I can't be hurt again. I can.
It's not that I can't feel emotion. I can.
But I can never be seriously damaged as
a woman ever again.'

♥

PART ONE

KATHLEEN TIMMINS was simply petite.

When I close my eyes, I see her... standing there, her hands joined in front of her tummy, and she is looking at me. Examining me in a way, but admiringly. With a nourishing pride, the way she always looked at me when I was a little girl.

She was a tiny woman. I have seen her wedding dress, I have held it in my hands and, honestly, it might fit on my thigh. The tiniest waist.

My eyes still closed, I see her in navy blue. When she came to visit us, she always wore a formal coat. Never black, and never the brightest colour either. A navy blue, I suppose, is the colour of the coat I choose for her when I imagine her... standing there.

Looking at me.

KATHLEEN TIMMINS was Gran Murphy to me.

My dad's mam.

The woman I am thrilled to be called after... Kathleen Timmins... Kathleen Murphy... Kathleen Chada.

Thankfully, we were both Kathleen Murphy for a period in our lives.

She had Irish blood in her veins, but Gran Murphy was born in England. She was raised in Birkenhead, a small town on the south bank of the River Mersey, opposite Liverpool, a city which was a home from home for so many Irish families needing work in the first half of the last century. And it was a search for work which brought the Timmins family to Birkenhead.

> *Life goes on day after day*
> *Hearts torn in every way*
> *So ferry 'cross the Mersey*
> *'Cause this land's the place I love*

When that song was in the charts, Kathleen Timmins wasn't working as a schoolteacher in Liverpool. She wasn't on that ferry daily.

She had given up her comfortable home in a big town many, many years before. A home that had running water, a toilet, electricity even. All the 'mod cons' that she didn't care too much remembering. Long before *Gerry and the Pacemakers* were singing about that ferry and the place they loved, Kathleen Timmins, now Kathleen Murphy, was living in a little stone cottage about two miles outside Tullow in County Carlow. When she first arrived, there was a pump outside, twenty yards from the back door.

The first thing her husband, William Murphy, put into the house for her was a cooker. Also waiting in the house for this newly married Englishwoman were two workmen. They were employed on the farm, and at night time there was a small ladder which allowed them climb over the new cooker, and lie down in an attic space that just about had enough room for two grown men.

Grandad Murphy, whom we all called 'Pop', was a little more austere, I remember, than his wife. He looked a strict man, but men back then dressed in their way and conformed, I guess, by looking sort of... *strict*. He wasn't alone with that 'look'.

He also had the nature of an entertainer. He was brilliant at doing animal shadows with his hands, and the room in which he and Gran Murphy lived their lives was made for all sorts of animals, big and small, appearing on the walls at night. Like most cottages, you entered the home through a little porch, with the kitchen to the right and living-room on the left. The oil cooker stood where once there had been an open fire, before William Murphy asked Kathleen Timmins for her hand in marriage. Before he wrote a letter to her mother and posed the question.

At night time, the entertainer in Pop Murphy came out.

He would fascinate us.

He was always seated to one side of the cooker, Gran Murphy on the other side... in her little rocking chair.

There was a press beside the warm cooker where we would sit, up on top of the press, where it was just so snug for us. I would curl up on top of that press for the whole evening, and just watch. Watch and listen. In the thick of it, but almost out of sight at the same time.

There was a lot of love in that small room.

Gran Murphy was a sweetheart. She was a 'gentle, gentle soul' everyone who knew her longer than I did, agrees. I was nine years old when Gran Murphy died, but I knew her, still, and knew her well enough to feel her presence in my life, even after she passed. She would come down to Ballinkillen to visit us once a week, or we would go to their house, on lots of Sundays.

I felt Gran Murphy more than Gran O'Reilly, who died when I was just five.

On the Murphy side of the family, I was the first grandchild.

Was I *spoiled*!!

I commanded whatever I wished, and I received far too much. As an infant, I could do no wrong, my mam has always told me.

When Gran Murphy arrived down to Ballinkillen, she would stand there, this tiny figure of a woman, and she would look at me. As soon as she came in the front door. Standing there, looking. Her hands by her side, and palms forward. Looking, and smiling.

She was quietly spoken, she didn't have a strong Liverpool

accent, but everyone could sense that Gran Murphy was a little different, tiny and a little more… foreign… exotic perhaps. She became pregnant with my dad, very quickly once married.

My mam tells the story that Gran Murphy was called back to Liverpool, quite soon after she was married. There was a family funeral at which she needed to be present. Her own mam wasn't one bit happy when she saw her daughter.

She thought her daughter was letting herself go.

She told her so.

Made it known to her daughter that she needed to go buy a corset.

Her own mam didn't realise that she was pregnant with my dad. It was 1933. My dad was born on December 23.

She had met my grandad when she had come home for a family reunion or some event, because the Timmins' had come from the same part of Carlow as the Murphys. She had come to Carlow regularly enough on holidays.

They met at a dance, though after that I have no idea how long their courtship lasted before marriage. They wrote to one another. In its day, theirs was a 'long distance relationship' until the day came when my grandad penned his letter formally asking for her hand.

My great gran Timmins sat down in Birkenhead, and replied, accepting the offer, once 'Kathleen is happy', she stressed. Our family still treasures that very letter, though my grandad's has disappeared.

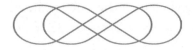

GRAN MURPHY had a stroke.

I remember going to Kilkenny hospital to visit her. She couldn't speak.

But I remember her crying as she lay there. She knew who we were, as we stood around her bed. I vaguely remember her funeral, though I have a clearer image of playing outside on the day she was buried in Tullow cemetery.

There was a ham salad meal for everyone, I can remember that too.

When Gran Murphy died, I never felt a great sense of loss. Because, I never believed I had lost her, I believed she was there for me, always, some form of… *Guardian Angel*, if you like?

Whenever I was in a stroppy mood as an older child, I would pound up the stairs in a huff, heading to my room, and I would sit on my bed.

'Nobody loves me!' I would announce quietly to myself.

The drama of it…

'Nobody loves me… only God and Gran!'

SOME MONTHS before Eoghan and Ruairi were taken from me, and murdered by their father, the man they trusted to protect them more than anyone else on this earth, Gran Murphy was with me.

It was around Christmas of 2012 when I was first aware of her presence. Eoghan and Ruairi were murdered the following July. The earliest hours of a Monday morning.

July 29.

Many months before that date, Gran Murphy was aware that something awful, a shattering happening awaited me in my life. I would wake up in the mornings and, immediately, I would feel her presence.

I didn't see her, I didn't hear her. I didn't feel anything physical.

We were back living in Ballinkillen, in a house newly built, and one Gran Murphy had never known or stood in.

For months and months through the first half of 2013, she was with me. This is not something that I have created in my own head. I can promise you it's not something that I imagined, something I subconsciously pieced together to calm myself in the immediate weeks and months after July 29.

My life seemed over. My being almost extinguished, but, I

know Gran Murphy was with me in the months prior to July 29 because I spoke to some of my colleagues at work about her. I was talking to one girl in particular at work about Guardian Angels.

She believed in Guardian Angels.

That's how our conversation began. And I told her that, for some reason, I was feeling my grandmother around me. Nearly all the time. And I told her it was not something that I was unhappy about; in fact I told her that it was lovely having her so close to me.

Gran Murphy was not with me after July 29.

Only before. At the time, I had no idea why.

But I now understand that Kathleen Timmins, that tiny woman from Birkenhead, a force of nature ten times her size, wanted me to know that she would be present for Eoghan and Ruairi when they passed from this life.

I'll be there for them.

Kathleen… I will mind your boys for you.

More than anything else, she wanted me to know that.

I think she smiled as Eoghan and Ruairi passed over, knowing that she was the presence they needed. Someone to offer them love and reassurance. We all felt so much pain over the boys' last moments, wondering how terrified they must have been.

I needed to know that my boys were in someone's arms, that they were being minded, and they were… by a beautiful tiny being, her arms open for them. I believe they passed over together.

Eoghan would have waited for Ruairi.

Eoghan died first, but he waited for his little brother.

IN THE early months of 2014, I was back at work at Sims IVF.

I was staying in Dublin, rather than driving up to Dublin and home to Carlow, and coming home to our large empty house on dark evenings. A friend's cousin had a B & B in Clonskeagh on the south of the city.

It was a small room I slept in, two or three nights each week. One morning, I woke up and said to myself... *Oh Gran, you're here!*

It was just that brilliant sense of her.

I passed the moment off and headed to work, and about an hour or two later I received a phone call that Uncle Tom, her son, was in hospital, he had taken a bad turn. He was in ICU. Uncle Tom passed away two weeks later.

After Uncle Tom passed, I had a conversation with her.

Now Gran, listen...

I really appreciate you being here for me, but...

I love you being with me.

But please don't do this anymore.

Every time you turn up, I'm thinking... who's next?

I don't need you to tell me... warn me, about anything... ever again.

Okay?

I love you Gran.

Gran Murphy has never returned to me.

When my time comes, maybe she will. Maybe she will stubbornly show up, unable to suppress her instinct to care for me. Mind me.

Others in our family have died since. My father, Billy passed away just as Covid hit in the spring of 2020. Billy Murphy, Gran Murphy's first child, the eldest of her six children.

She never came to me.

I believe Gran Murphy understands.

I BELIEVED Sanjeev Chada to be the love of my life.

He became my Sanj.

When we first met, I thought him quite handsome. I soon learned that he had a brilliant mind. I also believed him to be a good father. Kind and considerate, I thought. He was never an aggressive person. He was usually the peacemaker, if he was out with friends and there was any sign of an argument brewing. What I particularly liked about him was his calm demeanour, the easiness that he brought into my life and into so many situations in the early days. That changed as time went on. We had our ups and downs, like all couples, but we were pretty much similar in mind. Or so I thought.

I certainly believed that he loved me too.

We had known one another for so long, for so many years, seven years, eight years, before Eoghan was born. We were married for 10 years, though we were not 'lovey-dovey' in one another's company.

We didn't need to kiss in company, or tell each other how much we loved one another. Even on the day we got married, there was no over-the-top display of our love. We got married in Barbados. I actually wanted to cancel our wedding, because my dad was having a heart by-pass, but my parents were like… 'No, you're getting married!' The thought of me not getting married and having a child out of wedlock was something they did not wish to even contemplate.

Sanj didn't tell any of his friends what was happening. He didn't want some of them turning up unannounced. I didn't want his parents there, because if my parents were not present, *then*… it was just my decision, both families or none. But Sanj's parents had wanted to be there with us.

We had a list, before deciding on Barbados. We reached 200 names, and had some more still to go. Money was tight. We had just bought our first house. We were over in London for the weekend, with Sanj's parents, and we were walking down the street. We came across a travel agency and they were advertising wedding destinations.

I already had Barbados in mind.

We made up our minds. I didn't feel the need to walk down any aisle, and Sanj was happy with that. We went for it. The Almond Beach Hotel. Barbados.

We were supposed to get married in the hotel's gardens. But it had started raining that morning. It poured down. The garden was sopping wet. The beach was an option. I thought that tacky, getting married on a beach… *everyone watching?* I don't know why I thought that, or why the hotel garden was going to be any different to the beach

The Piano Bar was mentioned. And I thought it cool to be able to tell our grandchildren we were married in a bar!

They could place the garlands of flowers in there. Nobody else was in there. Again, we went for it. The hotel supplied a Minister. The wedding coordinator was one of our witnesses. The second witness was supposed to be our photographer, but he was in a car accident on the other side of the island.

The wedding coordinator doubled as our photographer.

Sanj wore a cream coloured suit. I didn't want a traditional wedding dress. I wore a dress I purchased in Laura Ashley… cream and maroon, and red shoes.

MY MAM and my dad were often mortifying.

They were so, so loving with one another. My mam is Patsy, Patsy O'Reilly. She had no trouble asking my dad for a kiss.

They would hold hands.

They would kiss… in public.

Oh my God… mam… dad!

Stop!!

My dad would sit at the top of the table, and my mam would always sit to his right. We'd all be sitting there after a family dinner, and mam would say… 'Give me a kiss!'

And we'd be like… 'Ohhhhh… Mammmmmmm!'

My dad would never refuse her request.

In their final years together, they would sit on the couch and they would hold hands. It was so beautiful.

They were so beautiful together.

MY DAD was a small man in height, only slightly taller than me. Maybe five feet five inches? Maybe slightly taller.

He was a little shorter than mam, I think?

My dad was the oldest of six children. My mam was the youngest of seven children.

Patsy O'Reilly grew up in Fruit Hill in Carlow, though she will correct me on that. Fruit Hill is actually in County Laois, and Carlow and Laois are particularly proprietorial about every inch of their land.

Her father passed when she was just 16 years old. Soon after, she travelled up to the Mater Hospital in Dublin to commence her training to be a nurse. When she completed her time, she came home to Carlow, to St Dympna's, a psychiatric hospital, and there she commenced a lifetime's work which included serving the community as a psychiatric nurse.

Patsy O'Reilly... now Patsy Murphy, was also a very strong woman, which complemented my dad's quieter, perhaps softer, character. There was nine years between them at birth.

They went out for quite some time, before dad managed to marry her and tie her down. My mam took her time before saying... 'Yes!'

Dad remained patient and persistent. He won out in the end. When they were engaged, my grandad, dad's dad, bought them a farm, a house and a farmyard, 50-odd acres all told in Ballinkillen near Bagenalstown.

Growing up, I can always hear my dad saying… '20 miles from Tullow, 15 miles from Carlow'… and the independence of living in Ballinkillen was just right for him, even though he was a strong family man and loved his brothers.

My dad knew what he wanted.

He was a very softly spoken man. Very, very patient.

And very gentle.

My mam, however, she was my Super Hero.

I always knew I wanted to be a nurse, because of mam.

In Ballinkillen, whenever anyone had a worry, they went to Patsy first, to my mam. If she couldn't help them, then they went to the chemist. If the chemist couldn't help, they went to the doctor.

It was easiest, and best, to go to Patsy Murphy to begin with.

I MET Sanj in Saudi Arabia.

In the spring of 1996 I took up a position in Riyadh.

The King Fahad National Guard Hospital was half an hour outside of the city. It was a general hospital and it was state-of-the-art, and huge. I absolutely loved it there, every single day, and I stayed for a total of seven years. I started off in orthopaedics, before moving to the surgical unit, and after that I was part of the VIP Outpatient's Clinic, which was a really lovely place to work. But where I really found my niche in the nursing world was in the Fertility Clinic, and I worked in IVF in Saudi for my last four years there.

It was 8pm-4pm Sunday to Thursday. Friday and Saturday was my weekend. The hospital was specifically for the members of the National Guard and their families, but the VIP Clinic was for officers and those higher up in the Guard. After that, there was the Royal Clinic which was exclusively for the Royal family.

The VIP Clinic was a busy place, and it looked a real hospital, with more marble than gold. It meant we were working on all aspects of care; medical, surgical, gynaecology, obstetrics, paediatrics... we were a good team, and I made some fantastic friends... Martina, Carrie, Tara, Mary!

I was over there 12 months, when I met Sanj.

Mary and I lived in a compound, in the hospital grounds, in a large and quite beautiful four-bedroom villa. It was perfect, relaxed, and without the bother of an 11pm curfew. We were lucky in the National Guard – we did not have that problem.

In lots of other hospitals off compound, you had to have friends, especially male friends you could trust, and who were happy to safely put you up for the night. I had the time of my life in Saudi Arabia. Everything about life was pretty great, including the money. I was a very happy ex-pat, and the unique lifestyle worked for me those seven years.

Mary was going out with a guy called Steve.

We were having a lunch party one afternoon, and Mary told me that Steve was bringing one of his friends… an Indian guy, she said.

He was good looking, I thought, when we first met.

We chatted, and connected pretty quickly, though I wasn't in the mood to go with the whole gang when they decided to bring the party to Steve and Sanj's house. I was working the next day.

Sanj said that if I was worried about getting home by curfew, that he would drive me to work the next morning. He told me I could sleep in his bed.

I didn't feel he was coming onto me.

In bed that night, we just talked. I didn't feel compromised in any way. We talked and talked, and I felt totally comfortable. We did kiss before going to sleep.

The next morning, he drove me to work as promised.

We met again at another party a few weeks later. There was nothing serious between us, but we were becoming friends. On New Year's Eve, however, an ex-girlfriend of his showed up at one of our parties and Sanj ended up leaving with her. That surprised me. He disappeared, and I was not impressed.

He hadn't even said goodbye.

He phoned me the next day to say that nothing had happened with her, that he had just been the gentleman dropping her off at her place. I believed him.

I was growing to really like his company. We talked about everything, and we talked about ourselves. He was brought up Hindu, I was brought up Catholic, and our family dynamics seemed very similar.

Soon, I had to confess to myself that I fancied him like crazy. I adored his brown eyes. But it was his easiness which attracted me more than anything. He was kind and considerate, and so relaxed with everyone. His mood seldom altered. He could hold his drink better than anyone, and he didn't smoke. He wasn't into drugs.

I couldn't understand why he had gone into accounting and banking because he was an outdoors person, and loved all sports. I never thought him suited to a desk job.

Six weeks in, we went on a short break to Hong Kong.

That cemented our relationship.

We were a pair. We loved talking, and we also loved the quiet times we had with our books. We both devoured books, especially thrillers and crime. We read one another's books all the time.

Also, we both loved good food.

It didn't matter that I was not a whizz in the kitchen. Sanj made up for the two of us, and he could handle anything, from a roast to the most sumptuous Indian dishes. I was to find out that his mam was an ever better cook.

And we both discovered that our son Eoghan had the same curiosity and passion. Eoghan loved his time in the kitchen with his dad.

MY MAM gave up nursing as a job when she got married, though she continued 'nursing' people all her life. That was the 'done thing' back then, women married and became full-time homemakers.

She also had a farm on her hands, however, at least until I was 11 or 12 and dad managed to buy additional acreage and a farmyard a couple of fields away.

Over time, the farmyard was moved over there. Some sheds were dismantled and brought down the road, and some remained around our house. Our home became less of a working farm.

Our house was in the middle of Ballinkillen, and there was not too much else in the village. A few more houses. The church across the road from our house, a shop down the road. There was a Community Centre, but there was no pub in Ballinkillen.

Social life was nearly all about 'visiting'.

Visiting uncles and aunts, and playing with cousins, or having them come to us. In Ballinkillen too, hurling was the No.1 piece of social business. Patsy O'Reilly, in her day, had been a handy camogie player, but my dad never played.

He was a horse man.

He adored his horses, though he hardly ever placed a bet. Billy Murphy could go to a race meeting and not put his hand into his pocket all day. A fiver placed on a horse was a rare moment; he just loved horses, and saw no need to gamble away his money on them. He inherited that love from his own dad, who had been into breaking horses as a younger man. Eoghan got his hurling skills from my mam, and his love of horses from my dad, I think.

One of the most dramatic days in my young life was when dad went to the sales in Goresbridge with his brother, Tom, who had a horse to sell. Dad ended up coming home with the same horse.

He landed in the yard with it, and I don't know if the horse was even broken. That day was the height of my dad's 'mid-life crisis', as we called it, that was as bad as it got… dad arriving home with his horse!

He hadn't even discussed it with my mother. She didn't believe it to be the worst thing in the world a husband could ever do!

After that, we ended up getting a pony we called Toby.

We all learned to ride on Toby, though I was terrified up there. One afternoon, however, I grasped my fear and saddled up Tony all on my own, with the intention of going for a short trot down the road.

The whole of tiny Ballinkillen was in immediate danger.

I couldn't handle him at all. He went into fields, he went into the school, he went wherever he wished.

I was the eldest in the family.

I was born on October 26, 1970. Next was Liam, a year and a half younger. He's living in Melbourne now. He went out there for a year, met Sharon who is Australian though of Maltese origin. They have two daughters, Sinéad and Molly, who are now young adults of 22 and 19 years of age, both born just a couple of years ahead of Eoghan and Ruairi.

Liam works in construction and owns machinery. He also owns some land, and horses. The Murphys will always love their horses!

Ken was next. He and his wife, Jean, who is from South Africa, are both chefs. They met while working on the QE2, but have brought their skills back home and own three cafes in Cork. They have three children, Ciarán (15), Samantha (12) and Gemma (nine). Then there was Kevin. He lives in Ballinkillen, after taking over the farm from dad.

Kevin and Triona have two, Hannah (13) and William (11)... the line of William Murphys is not stopping any time soon!

My youngest brother is Brian, a fitter, who is married to his childhood sweetheart, Orla. They've been blessed with four; Sarah is 15 (she was born six days after Ruairi, and they were best buddies), Holly is 13, Olivia is 11, and Evelyn, who would buy and sell all of my nieces and nephews, is five.

Finally, there's my sister Irene... 10 years younger than me. Irene and Donal have twin girls, Emily and Rachel, who are 13, and Adam who is 11.

Ciarán, Sarah and Ruairi... we used to call them the Three Musketeers!

I love all of my nieces and nephews dearly. They are my joy.

I get big hugs and kisses from them all... and lots of 'I love you, Auntie Kathleen!', before they are gone out of sight!

But I cherish having each of them in my life.

MY PARENTS did all of their practising on how to raise a child, on me.

I was the eldest, but I was still allowed to be a child. There was not any huge expectation placed on me, at least none that I was aware of growing up. And because there were four boys straight after me, that meant I was closer still to mam.

The boys were all ready to be outside doing their bit.

Me?

The most I would do is stand in a gap, if my help was very badly needed. I was never the outdoorsy type. The boys would feed the calves. I would cook.

Saturdays for mam and me was all about baking and cooking. Baking tarts and buns, that was me, and I soon found out that I could actually make a nicer pastry than mam, who said I had a lighter touch. That was me on my way, or so I thought.

My first customer was Mrs Byrne's down the road. She had a small shop in the village, which is now known as Tim's, her son's. But I had an arrangement with Mrs Byrne.

It began when I started saving for a trip to Lourdes, and I took my buns to Mrs Byrne's. She sold them for me.

And we had a good run on our buns, and we even survived

one St Patrick's weekend, when I thought it a good idea to colour our buns... green. One of my best customers brought his bag of buns back to Mrs Byrne, and was firmly of the opinion that his favourite buns were gone all mouldy.

I still haven't made it to Lourdes!

OUR LOCAL paper, the *Nationalist* had an advert for nurses' training in London. In Kingston-Upon-Thames. Kingston General.

My friend, Teresa was applying.

Sure, I might as well, I thought. Mam drove up to the Skylon Hotel on Drumcondra Road in Dublin. There was an aptitude test, and an interview after the exam. I knew coming home that I had my place.

It was March of 1988, three months before my Leaving Cert.

Now I won't have to do the Leaving!

Mam thought otherwise.

I was due to start my training the following April but, that summer, I decided to go over to London. I had written to the hospital to see if they had any nurses' aid positions? While I was awaiting a reply, someone from the hospital phoned my house in Carlow with the good news. I came home and did some extra packing.

I started that July.

I wasn't turning 18 till the following October. I knew so little. But I was able to get the ferry, and get a bus to Euston. My cousin, John, collected me and drove me to the hospital. I was given a small room in the nurses' home.

A single bed, a locker, a wardrobe and a tiny desk. Just me… Teresa had decided not to go over, and did her training in Dublin instead.

I would sleep in that same room for three years, but the home was really nice, and so close to Richmond Park, just walking distance. From night one, I don't remember feeling worried, or at all daunted at what lay ahead.

I was a little lonely, but mostly excited.

I had a blue and white uniform to wear, with buttons up the centre. There was only a half-mirror in my room, but, there I was, ready, on my way, a Super Hero in Training… in Patsy O'Reilly's slipstream.

I had no little hat. Only student nurses got to wear those, a little white paper hat, with one stripe for first year, two for second year, three for third year.

Those hats would prove such a nuisance, and a health hazard.

That lay ahead of me.

I had so much to learn.

Baby-sitting in Ballinkillen was the only skill I possessed.

A big world outside Ballinkillen awaited me, and also my first real boyfriend. Some of the girls I worked with thought I needed a boy in my life fast. He was a third year student. His name was Nick, he was from Blackpool. He was lovely, and kind, and for my 18th birthday he went and bought me a little fridge for my room. It fitted neatly under my desk. I had a kettle, you see, but I hadn't anywhere to keep the milk for my tea.

As Nick was also working in the hospital, he was able to stay over with me and no questions were ever asked. The nurses' home wasn't that strict about that sort of thing, anyway.

Nick was very quiet. He wasn't really a drinker, and as neither of us had all that much money we didn't go out very often. The cinema now and again, but we mostly stayed in my room watching telly. I had a fridge, a kettle and a telly, and Nick went and bought me a car.

He was so good to me.

But because we were together so soon after I landed in London, I never got to really experience the city, or explore the other side of student life. It was 40 pence for a soda water and lime, when I did go to the pub, and occasionally I might nurse a West Coast Cooler for most of the evening.

I never really got to learn how to drive in the creamy yellow car, as a couple of months later I broke it off with Nick. And broke his really good heart. I felt I was just too young. I told him face-to-face, in my room. Then, of course, he broke my heart right back a couple of weeks later when I found out he was dating another student nurse. Before then, he took the car back... and dead right too!

I actually didn't end up getting my full driving licence until I was 32! I failed one test in England, and I also failed in Ireland when I came home.

But I loved Kingston General.

I was confident about myself, and my decision, from day one almost. We would do a rotation while training, 16 weeks on, and three weeks off. And I came home to Ballinkillen for those three weeks every time.

After qualifying, I only stayed one more year over there, I'm not sure why. They were so kind and supportive, especially so early on when my first patient died on me. He was an elderly man. He was in a side ward in the unit, and I was unaware that he had passed.

'Kathleen, can you come here please!'

The head nurse discovered the poor man early that morning. I was so shocked, and upset. But that's why even Super Heroes have to go into training, I suppose.

SANJ WORKED in Saudi Arabia for four years.

He left well before me, but he was also the reason I finally decided to quit the ex-pat life too. I was 30 years of age at that time.

Sanj 'brought' me home.

We had been together in Riyadh for three and half years as a couple. He had been working for Citibank, but after doing his first three years, and taking up the option of an additional 12 months, his plan always was to go travelling, with his friend, Hugh. The pair of them had initially spent some time travelling on a shoestring after they left college, and topping up on this experience, before finally settling down, was important to them. And this time, they were going to do it with money in their pockets.

As someone who is 'not' a backpacker, I was never going with them. But I always knew it was in their plans. It was never an issue between us.

They left in the middle of the summer, but a couple of months before that I walked into the room as Sanj was writing an email. He was talking about a meeting with friends the following Christmas, in Thailand, and it was clear to me that I was not invited to that. Either that, or he forgot to mention me.

I got quite upset with him.

And I made up my mind that, as soon as he left Riyadh, we were finished with one another. We had been living together all those years but, obviously, in Saudi you cannot officially be living together unless you are married. So we shared houses all the time during those years and I stayed over, usually in his place. It was a nice compound outside of the city. I was happy staying there with him.

As we talked about his email, there were tears.

I walked away from him, and he followed me. It was the first time we ever had 'words' with one another. 'You don't want me with you!' I told him, or something of that order... 'I know I'm not travelling with you, but you don't want me with you after that!'

We had never actually talked about the future, or 'our' future, and I just think it was something that neither of us had put much thought into up to that point. I think it might have been a bit of a shock to him, to finally be having such a conversation... about 'us'.

I remember him saying, 'Well, no... you don't need an invitation!'

He left that summer.

We had made the decision that we would continue our relationship, at a distance as he travelled. We decided we'd meet up, when it suited us both, and as I had the money working in Saudi I was able to get to see him. He started off in Germany, and then Hugh and himself did Vietnam and Cambodia, and they were in Thailand as planned for Christmas.

I joined them there, Sanj and Hugh, and some other people we knew well. While his travelling continued, I spent about two more years in Riyadh, before finally it was time for me to come home to Ireland. I came back in 2002. By then, Sanj was 'home' and working in London.

He wasn't back in banking, it was a temporary job, and he was living with his mam and dad. This was the first time that I felt the dynamic had changed in our relationship. He was pushing me to come back. We had been about two years apart and, I believe, if our relationship had ended at that point, I would have been saddened. But not devastated.

While he was on the move, I might have had only one phone call with him. There were no mobile phones back then, or very few… there was no WhatsApp. It was expensive at that time to make calls, but there were cyber cafes, everywhere.

We did have email in the hospital. Even my colleagues at work would comment on it, when I hadn't heard from Sanj for a period of time. I was fine for three days or so, but after day four or five, then I would get a bit antsy, and after that… the girls could tell that I was in bad form. And they knew when he'd emailed me – I marched into work in the best of form!

AFTER BREAKING up with Nick, I was seeing another guy in London, a Dubliner called Andy. He was also a lovely, kind man. He was a good few years older than me, six years I think, but I felt I was incredibly lucky with the men in my life... Nick, Andy... and then Sanj and I also got to know one another.

I was 21, and we ended up staying together for two years, but my time in London came to an end more suddenly than I had imagined it would. I had come home to Ballinkillen in early December, because I was working over Christmas that year.

When the time came to go back to London, I was overcome with sadness, and I had never felt like that before. I had a ritual each time I left Ballinkillen for London, a ritual that had been in place for four years. My mam always brought me to the airport.

I would say goodbye to my dad at the door of the house, and we'd get into the car and go down the road to the shop, Mrs Byrne's. I would pop in and say goodbye to her also, I'm not sure why, but I think she always reminded me of my Gran Murphy, in a way, and besides she had always been so kind and loving to me.

This particular afternoon, Mrs Byrne cried as I was leaving.

And then, I cried from that moment until I got back into my house in London. It was the week before Christmas, and arrivals at the airport was choc-a-bloc with people coming home that bit early. Departures was virtually empty.

All I could see were all of these people so happy to be coming home, and here was I going in the wrong direction. Andy couldn't understand why I was so upset. I finished with him quickly after that, as I needed a clean break. In fairness, it was a bit of a shock to him. It was the final week of 1992. I was back home in 1993, and registered with the Irish Nursing Board.

However, because I was so upset, at work they would not accept my notice initially. But soon enough, I was packing up my things in the old style Georgian house I was sharing, that looked magnificent from the outside, but was unloved and really old on the inside. I had been living on the top floor, where there was an annex, so it was like my own living space with a bedroom attached. My brother and my cousin came over in a car, and they helped me load up all my stuff for the big return back to Ballinkillen.

I was home less than six weeks, when I started working in Navan, in Our Lady's Hospital. This was 30 years ago, pre-internet. I remember, I was in Navan with my cousin and I popped into the hospital to see if they had any jobs, and I was offered work that same night. I told the Matron I had nothing with me.

She looked at me, and told me I'd have enough time to get the bus back to Dublin and be back in Navan to begin a seven o'clock shift!

I said I couldn't.

But, I did start the very next night in Navan. That was me, a young nurse seeing the world through rose-tinted glasses, wanting to save everyone, and give everyone all the care and love *in the world*.

Navan did give great care to its patients, but the hospital itself was from a different time and place, and after working in England it was like travelling back in time a century or so. It broke my heart. I remember talking with one mother and daughter about this man, their loved one who had dementia. I had so many ideas, so much that could be done for him through community care. They told me they had nothing. They had to lock the sitting-room door to keep him inside, to keep him safe.

On call for the ambulance service, you could end up anywhere, in a house, at a road accident, you never knew, and although I was a qualified nurse, I was still only 23 years of age and someone with no first aid experience at trauma events. I was used to having qualified people to my left and right in London. In Navan, it was sometimes me and an ambulance driver, but the ambulance drivers in Navan were amazing and knew what they had to do.

THE PHOTO on the front cover of this book was taken on a Friday morning. By me. But it was early in the morning, before the boys went off to school, and trying to get them to hold still and stick together, tight, was not easy.

Eoghan was in Third Class. Ruairi in Senior Infants.

It was April, another school year would soon be over.

Three months later, they would be taken from me.

I was after buying a little photo-frame for my sister-in-law and I was struggling to find what to put into it and, quickly, I thought I'd take a photo of Eoghan and Ruairi. I'd get it sized and into the frame.

The messing from them that particular morning…

It was 'no uniform' day in Ballinkillen school, so they were wearing purple, in their local soccer club, Nurney Villa hoodies. Eoghan played, and Ruairi hadn't started yet, but he still wanted the jersey, same as his big brother. Anything his big brother did, Ruairi wanted to do. Ruairi was so giddy. He kept pushing Eoghan.

It was almost 8.30. It was only a kilometre or so to the school, but I always drove them.

'Would you both STOP!' I said, laughing with them.

'I have to take this photograph!'

IRENE AND I were 10 years apart in age.

Twice the age difference of Eoghan and Ruairi.

My little sister was an irritating little madam, who just annoyed me. But this was when she got this little bit older and bigger.

When I was 17 and heading off to London to nurse, Irene was only seven years old. It was when she was two and three, that she was the *annoying* little sister. To begin with, I could not wait to have a sister, of course. I remember hearing that she was born, and then going to see her. *The excitement!* She's the only one of my siblings who I can remember being brought to Kilkenny Hospital… *to see!* My dad had woken me that morning, and told me. Mam brought me down to the nursery in the hospital and there she was, our little baby… *my little sister!*

And she was this little doll, for the first two or three years.

Before she would start telling tales.

Before she'd want things that were… *Mine!*

All the time, she wanted everything and she wanted to get her way. And I spent more on Irene than I did on myself at the same time. I would buy her dresses, in Marks and Spencer… and Laura Ashley. She was… *My little Doll.* I think she enjoyed being that little doll, too, for a while.

EOGHAN IN that photo, with his long hair!

He always had his hair short.

Sanj had long hair like that too, but when I met him first he wore his hair short. He grew his hair out when he was not working in an office.

Eoghan would have chats with Sanj, about his dad's long hair, and tell him… 'Only girls wear long hair!'

But at one point, maybe when he was about eight, Eoghan didn't want to have his hair cut. He would go into the barber in Bagenalstown alright, but he would insist that he only needed it trimmed.

Ruairi's hair, in contrast, was really thick and dead straight, and when he came home from the barbers it was like he was wearing a helmet on top of his head.

Eoghan's was thinner, with a slight curl to it.

At one point, Sanj and I decided we had to have a conversation with Eoghan. He had his hair in a ponytail when he played soccer, and we warned him that other boys might have a go at him, tease him. He had finer features than Ruairi, and could have been mistaken for a girl. He had beautiful features to his face.

That did happen a few times.

But that never bothered him. Eoghan told us that if other boys made that mistake, and thought that they would have it easier playing against a girl, then, it would be a help to him.

'It might not work like that!' I warned him.

'They'll call you a girl on purpose!'

For his 10th birthday, he joined Borris Golf Club. A big present! He was mad about golf. He had started playing a couple of years earlier, and actually took some lessons with Sanj, from a pro. A place in Carlow did 'parent and child' lessons. Eoghan and Sanj also played together that year as often as they could.

I think the golf improved Eoghan's hurling... and the hurling helped his golf. He had also started a golf camp that summer he died. And one of the instructors said something to someone else, about 'the girl'. About having a 'girl' there! Eoghan overheard.

He was so confident within himself, so *quietly* confident.

'I'm not a girl,' he calmly informed the men. 'My name is Eoghan!'

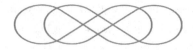

I NOW have my little sister as my best friend in the world.

We are so close.

We are all so close in our family, me, Irene and my four brothers. Our upbringing was incredibly grounded and solid. I knew we were loved. We all knew, it was a love that was life-affirming.

We didn't have lots of money, and there were times when things were tough on us all. I was about 14 or 15, when many in dad's herd of cattle got TB.

He recovered financially. But it almost wiped him out.

I have this memory of him, sitting in the kitchen... in tears.

I didn't feel I was in a position to say anything to him... or comfort him. I just watched him, and felt my own heart break for him. He lost about two-thirds of his herd, I think.

And I remember my mam saying to me once, that she and dad were never as well off as the day they both had their pension, because it was the only time in their lives that they had a regular income. My dad did some other work for others farmers, ploughing and spraying, but as a child you are never aware if there is money. I never saw them arguing... mam and dad. Though, we all knew when mam was cross.

Because dad would go quiet.

I OFTEN wonder if Eoghan would have kept his hair long?

What would he look like now, as a 20 year-old man?

He didn't want his hair long in order to stand out. He didn't need to do that. Eoghan had a quiet confidence, which was one of his strengths. I could see that about him, since he was about six.

One of his teachers told me.

That Eoghan had this special ability to 'bring out' a shy or quieter boy or girl, and a great ability to calm others down. She always knew, she told me, where to sit him in the class. Where he could help her best.

Already, he had this maturity. And I think he got this from me, more than his father. Initially, when the boys were born, I sometimes felt a little intimidated by the fact that Sanj was a very clever person, and that he had been rewarded academically.

He had gone to college, and I had gone to nursing school. I'm not taking away from myself or any nurses. We do what we feel we are destined to do in this world, and I've met so many nurses with the most brilliant minds.

We all make our choices in life.

I 'saw' Sanj as being the clever one and while he never said anything like that to me, at the same time he did not stop me from telling family, others, just how brilliant he was.

Eoghan was bright. I could see that.

He and Ruairi took everything they had from both of us. And also from the place in which they grew up, and the people in that place. They grew up in the village of Ballinkillen and they were surrounded by my family. They would see Sanj's family now and then.

The greatest love they knew came from us in Ballinkillen, which was just naturally the way it was...

WE HAD our squabbles. Squabbles, which for children and teenagers, can present themselves as World War Three. We'd want to watch different things on telly. Someone might want to sit on someone else's chair and, when that person got up… the other would pounce.

WAR!

We all went to the same national school down the road. The same school my boys, Eoghan and Ruairi, would also attend. I then went to Presentation De La Salle in Bagenalstown, mainly because all my friends were going there. The boys, and Irene, they all went to the Technical School in Borris. The school in Bagenalstown was only five miles away. The school bus travelled through Ballinkillen.

Our house was in the middle of the street, and the bus literally went right past our front door. I would get up in the morning, inevitably late… and first thing, I'd put my bag outside the front door. Where it could be seen by the bus driver, when he was coming down the road.

I'd go back inside, and get ready and have my breakfast.

Once he saw my bag, the driver would stop and beep on his horn, patiently, too patiently. I'd still be wolfing down my breakfast.

Looking back, all he ever had to do, just the once, was to drive by the house… drive by my lonely school bag. But he never did.

That would have put manners on me, fast.

EOGHAN WAS such a loving boy.

I speak about Eoghan more than Ruairi, because his personality was being formed more at 10 years of age, and I could *see* him.

Ruairi had such a big personality for such a small kid, but it was different with him. I didn't have enough time with him, to imagine his future in quite the same way as Eoghan's. And that is why I talk about Eoghan a little bit more.

I am conscious of this.

And I struggle with it a bit.

Eoghan was developing, and taking up more of my attention, but it was something that would have balanced itself out over time. If the three of us had… *more time.*

Between the pair of them, however, even in the short period of their lives, there was always a strong sense of right and wrong, and justice. One wasn't dominant over the other. And they took turns doing things.

They worked it out quite well, *themselves.*

I remember going to a parent-teacher meeting. My last such meeting, and I discussed why Eoghan had been given detention. This was the first time we had heard anything like this about Eoghan. He had been with three other boys. They were all in the same trouble. Some other boy was acting up and messing, and annoying them, so they decided not to pick him on whatever team they were picking.

Their teacher said that Eoghan and the others were right, but that he still had to be seen to punish them a little bit. But Eoghan had been mortified coming home the day it had happened. He only had to stay in the classroom during lunchtime. That was tough for boys who wanted to play football, but that wasn't what upset Eoghan at all.

Sanj texted me at the time… *You'll never guess what happened?*

I was in Dublin, at work, and a few minutes later I had Eoghan phoning me. I knew he was a good boy. Like all kids, there were times when he would drive us demented. But he was a *good* boy.

He called me 'Mam'.

But he called Sanj… 'Mate'.

Either 'Dad' or 'Mate'.

That's what stays with me.

Sanj and Eoghan were friends.

Eoghan was a mini Sanj.

He wanted to be him, and because his daddy called his friends 'Mate', in that English way, Eoghan wanted to be mates with his dad too.

Sanj knew that.

And that's what makes it all so terrible, so heart-breaking. He did not kill his son, and just his son. He killed his son, his friend, his 'Mate'.

Sanj saw that 'mini me' in Eoghan. And it makes it all the

harder to think of them in that way. In the months before Eoghan was murdered by his father, he had been calling him 'Mate' all the time.

They had been calling one another 'Mate'.

I THINK I had a crush on this boy in school.

My friends told me I had a crush on him, so I believed them. Whether I did or not, I have no idea.

He wasn't the first boy I kissed, though, that was someone else at the school disco, whose name I cannot remember. I do remember that he kissed one of my best friends the next week. At discos, our parents would drop us off and collect us.

So, that always put manners on us a bit, though it was better when dad collected me. 'Please, please dad… collect me tonight!' I would ask him.

Mam, you see, would always get there early when she was collecting, and she'd park right outside the front door. She was the first person I would see when I walked out. There was the occasional, 'Did I see you walking… ?'

'No mam… no, that wasn't me!' I'd tell her.

I DON'T believe I was a rebellious child.

But I did put my foot down in my teens, far too early, when it came to religion.

I decided I didn't believe in God.

So why should I go to Mass anymore?

Decision made!

I was in class one day, soon after, when the teacher called me out. Fr Dowling, our parish priest, who has since passed away, was waiting to have a word with me.

About what?

My mother, the church sacristan, had decided to put a stick in the wheels of my revolt, and asked him to have a word. This was a *big* one, for me.

I knew the biggest reason I didn't want to go to Mass was that I had to get up so early on Sunday mornings, but I wasn't going to say *that* to Fr Dowling.

He was actually quite nice to me.

I wasn't able to explain my thinking to him.

I backtracked.

'Why did you go and do that?' I asked my mother, the minute I got home.

The church was literally across the road from our house.

I ended up making the short walk the next Sunday.

That, I believe, was as rebellious as I got as a teenager.

Once my sister came along, I began sharing my bedroom with her. It was a three-bed house, and the boys had their room, the four of them. My room was girly, and stayed that way with Irene around.

I had Harlequin Clown wallpaper, and it is still there on the walls of the room. Clowns, with peaked caps, and tears. Clowns, and 'Duran Duran'. That was me.

The rebel without a cause.

EOGHAN AND Ruairi were proud of their skin colour.

I don't believe there was an awareness, per se; they just knew that they were a little bit different, and they celebrated that fact.

They got a lot of... 'look at those gorgeous eyes, and dark skin!'

Of course they both liked that.

They didn't look Indian, as such, but more Mediterranean, like their dad in the early days when I first met him. They had that sallow look. When his hair was short, most people thought Sanj was Italian.

Ruairi was slightly darker than Eoghan.

The first school photo of Ruairi's, I noticed that, but we still had to be really careful that they never got too much sun, because they burned easily with that sallow skin.

Eoghan was quite fascinated about his Indian origins.

We went over to England as often as we could, and Eoghan was very close to his grandfather, Kamal. I would have liked him and Bimla, Sanj's mother, to speak more Punjabi to Eoghan, but they seldom did. I thought it would have been very good for him to learn some of the language.

Bimla still lives in Essex.

I have always called her Mrs Chada. I was never invited to call her Bimla, for some reason, even though all of my family call her Bimla.

Kamal passed away when I was pregnant with Ruairi. So, Ruairi never knew his grandfather, and Eoghan had such a short time with him. But they were good years, and Kamal was a very hands-on grandad. He loved getting down on the floor and playing with Eoghan.

He had two granddaughters at the time Eoghan was born, but I knew how excited he was with the arrival of his first grandson.

The family went 'home' to India to bring his ashes to his final resting place, and Sanj was gone for those two or three weeks. Eoghan was only five, but he was fascinated at what was happening, and he had so many questions about his grandfather.

As the boys got older, I know they would have wanted to explore their family heritage more, and I'm sure they would have travelled to India lots to begin with. I know they both would have loved finding out more.

Kamal was a big, strong presence in his family's life, and in Sanj's life. If his dad was still alive, I absolutely believe that Sanj would never have murdered our boys.

Sanj would not have wanted to disappoint his father.

He would not have dared take his grandson away from Kamal. I honestly feel the one person Sanj loved and respected more than anything in this world was his father. He was a very fit and healthy man, who had worked hard all of his life. He worked for Ford until the day he retired. His death was too early, and sudden. He was still in his early seventies.

His passing was a big blow to everyone. Eoghan took part in the funeral and he was very good the whole time. Indian funerals can be very overpowering, loud and flamboyant compared to our funerals in Ireland, and there is a lot of wailing. But Eoghan was okay with everything.

My mam was over with us, and if we thought things were too much for him, she was there to take him away for a while. As a grandson, there were things for him to do, as he was coming down the 'male line' of the family, and he didn't mind putting objects into the coffin beside his grandad.

PART TWO

WHEN HIS time came, my dad was one of the lucky ones.

It was Easter, 2020, and the country was beginning to live with Covid. My dad had chest problems for as long as we can all remember, and we credit our local doctor in Bagenalstown, Dr Tom Foley for keeping him alive for as long he did. Billy Murphy had COPD (Chronic Obstructive Airways Disease). He was 86 when he died.

That Easter, dad was admitted to hospital in Kilkenny.

My mam's brother-in-law, Uncle Phonsus, passed away with Covid in the early weeks of the pandemic here in this country; his was one of the first 'Covid funerals'. He died in hospital.

There was no dignity afforded him; he was wrapped in sheets, in what he was wearing in the hospital, placed into a bag, and then placed into a sealed coffin, and brought directly to the graveyard.

He died all alone, and he was buried with the minimum number of people present to say their goodbyes. I was about to drive mam and dad to the graveyard, on the strict understanding that they would not get out of the car, but I received a phone call from mam on the Easter Monday telling me that dad had taken another 'turn'.

He had many turns. Each occasion, he would pass out. Dad

would be unresponsive, and we'd call an ambulance, get him into hospital, where he would receive antibiotics and steroids, and he'd come around again.

This time, because of everything that was happening with Covid and hospitals, it was agreed that we'd take our time on getting him admitted, and we'd wait and see. I had an emergency supply of antibiotics and steroids from Dr Tom, and we used these over the weekend. I gave him a double dose, and kept an eye on him.

I travelled to my uncle's funeral on my own, and I was passing by so many people who were out on the road, kindly paying their respects. I found that so emotional, but then, suddenly, I received a phone call from my sister-in-law, Orla, telling me that dad was not very well at all and that they thought they needed to call an ambulance immediately. She explained that it seemed like dad had had a bad reaction to 'something'.

I headed off back down the road in a panic, thinking... *Oh my God, I've killed him.*

I've given him too much of the antibiotics, the steroids... I've killed him.

It was only when the ambulance arrived that we found out that the previous night, dad had fallen. He was on a divan bed and he slipped off the edge of it onto the ground. He got back up with the help of mam, and he hadn't complained of any pain through the night, or the next morning, but in the fall he had collapsed one of his lungs.

The reaction he experienced was his body filling up with fluid.

This was the first time neither mam nor I could travel with dad to the hospital. We were devastated watching him being taken away from us.

For mam, not being able to go into hospital to see him in the days that followed was crippling. She had 10 tough days before dad returned home.

He was, as I've already said, one of the lucky ones.

He didn't catch Covid while he was in hospital, which was incredible, and he was back home with his loved ones who could all take care of him. He didn't last long.

But all of his children were with him, and he got to speak on the phone with my brother in Australia. He also got to chat with his own brother. Everybody who was important in his life.

We all said goodbye to dad.

In the end, mam knew he was going.

He went to bed about 11.30pm that final night, and mam locked the doors and followed him. She knew by his colour that something was wrong. She helped him lie down... she knew...

'Oh Billy, don't leave me... don't go!' she pleaded.

Quickly, however, she stopped.

She knew it was his time. Mam composed herself.

'If it's time, Billy,' she told him, kissing him on the forehead, 'go in peace.'

She called us all to come and say our goodbyes.

Billy Murphy didn't receive a wake that he deserved, and because he was so loved, due to Covid. But he would have enjoyed our goodbye even more, because as a family we all came together with our kids.

His grandkids were there, and his youngest granddaughter at the time was only three years old. She was running around his coffin, and darting underneath. William, his grandson, was nine and as I walked by the room late into the night I saw William with dad... William's hand on Billy Murphy's hand.

It was something beautiful to witness.

All the little girls, a whole row of them against the wall, stayed with him too, talking and telling him how much they loved him and how they would miss him.

Dad was lucky.

We were all so lucky.

Dad was a fantastic father, but I always said he was born to be a grandfather. And, just like Gran Murphy, he was happiest just sitting back and watching his grandchildren.

'Isn't it great!' he'd say to mam.

I imagine him looking down on us all these days, seeing everyone he loves together... thinking to himself... *Isn't it great!*

I <u>KNOW</u> that mam and dad's greatest fear, after Eoghan and Ruairi were taken from me, was that I would end my own life.

Only I knew that was not going to happen.

My boys were gone, but I continued to live with their presence.

I had that, and if I didn't have *that*, the *sense* that they were still with me, what would have been the point in continuing to stay alive?

I had everything taken from me. My boys… and Sanj was in prison. It took me time to comprehend the evil he had done, and understand *what* he had been in my life, but he was gone too. From July 29, 2013, I was alone.

I have looked at others who have lost their children, and I know it is always the most awful thing, but I can't help thinking that they still have one another as husband and wife. Before Eoghan and Ruairi were murdered, friends of mine, Irene and David, had lost their beautiful little daughter, Alana. She had been killed in a tragic car accident a few weeks before Christmas. I remember them telling me at the time, explaining why they had to get up out of bed and continue with their family life. Alana's big brother had a birthday to celebrate in early December. They still had to make sure that Santa came too.

Their words after Eoghan and Ruairi's deaths were so inspirational – they understood the hurt and pain, but also *understood* the need to carry on.

I felt I had nothing left in my life after that Sunday in July, and it might have appeared that I had nothing to keep me going, but I had Eoghan and Ruairi, I *had*… and I *have*, and I found my reason to continue living in my love for my boys.

I also had mam and dad.

I never wanted my mam and dad to go through what I was going through. Even though I was an adult, I was still their daughter, I was still their child. I could not knowingly put them through anything more, how could I?

That's what kept me going; that and knowing their greatest fear in the months and years after the boys were taken from me. This was brought home to me, forcefully, two days before the first anniversary of Eoghan and Ruairi's deaths.

I was in the house on my own that night, when I got a really bad pain in my side. I'd had my gall bladder removed years before, so I had no idea what was wrong. I had to phone my sister-in-law, who was a nurse with Caredoc at the time, but there was nothing she could do to relieve the pain. We decided we should go to Caredoc, but she had been out earlier in the night and so neither of us could drive. We phoned my brother, Brian, and he phoned mam to tell her that they were bringing me to the doctor.

'Oh my God… what's she done?'

Those were my poor mam's words, that was her immediate thought. Brian told me this, and I had to make it my business a few days later to sit down with mam and assure her that I would never do… *anything.*

'I know you worry, and I understand,' I told her, 'but I will never do that… I promise!'

Around the same time, I also remember talking it through with my psychologist, and telling him that I had no idea what would happen, or if anything would change, when mam and dad were also gone from my life.

I know that when dad died, I struggled.

I did really struggle, and I needed help, and I was admitted to St Patrick's Hospital. But it was my choice to be admitted, which was so important to me.

My Choice!

I WAS speaking with my psychologist about what my life would be like when one or both of my parents were gone. They were my family; I didn't have a partner, and I didn't have children anymore, so, they were my *family*.

My brothers and my sister had their own immediate families, besides mam and dad.

Dad had been a huge presence in all of our lives, even if he was a quiet, strong presence. I was so close to him, and his death brought me right back to the earliest days after I had lost Eoghan and Ruairi. Covid, too, was a lonely time for everyone in the country.

Suddenly, I was not working, and I was in my house all of the time, and mostly alone. I was in a bubble with my mam. Getting back to work after an initial six-weeks period was amazing, and helped, and I had an outlet again, and I got through the summer. But I knew I was slipping.

I could not lift myself.

Everything in my life was grey, or black.

I would sit for hours watching television, but I had no idea half of the time what exactly I had been watching. I was largely inactive.

I had no energy. I didn't want to talk to anybody. I had to force myself to do... *anything*.

Losing dad had been the trigger.

Another loss in my life.

I spoke to Dr Tom, and he put me back on anti-depressants, and I was also seeing my psychologist more regularly, and we talked everything through, every time. It was he who suggested that it might be a good time to 'go in' somewhere?

The anti-depressants were doing their job, although it took a few different tries before I happened upon the right ones. However, they took the edge off *everything* I was living, the pain, and also all the good parts of my life.

It was like I was living in the clouds, and not really doing anything, or even thinking very much.

But the clouds were a better place than living in the dark... in that dark, *dark* place. Physically, it felt like I was holding onto myself tightly... so tight, and that I was afraid of letting go in case I shattered once I allowed myself to feel any emotion.

Shattering into pieces.

That terrified me, and I was afraid I was going to fall into an even darker, deeper hole. And never be able to get out of it. At times, I also wondered if I could muster up the energy any more to keep fighting it.

St Pat's in Dublin was suggested for a period of time? It was described to me as a 'safe place to fall apart', and then be put back together again.

What I subsequently found out was that I did not fall apart. I could be emotional, I could cry... and not fall apart. And I also discovered in St Pat's that I had the ability to actually put myself back together again if I did begin to crack a little.

I discovered also that it was okay to be emotional. I could do so, without going into an even darker place.

My brother brought me to the hospital.

As I walked through the front doors, I felt nothing but sheer relief. It was immediately after Christmas. The previous October, my cousin Claire had taken her own life. I was by the river, with her family, when her body was recovered from the water.

But in the search for Claire, I had felt the cracks widen, lengthen.

It was like I was being transported back in time to that Sunday in July 2013, and the days that followed.

My brothers helping to look for Claire.

The anguish, and the horror of not knowing, displayed on every face.

Claire's family being asked to identify her body.

Her sister bravely saying, 'I'll do it'.

A guard saying, 'No, I'll ask one of the lads!'

I had been here before.

As I stood there, I experienced such a flood of different emotions, but one in particular stood out, a thought that was loud in my head, that Claire had escaped.

And I felt envious.

Her pain was gone.

It was at that moment that I finally realised I did need to 'go in' somewhere.

As it was the first Christmas since dad had passed, I did not want to be in hospital that week. I went into St Pat's on December 27. Again, as it was in the middle of Covid, there were going to be no visitors for however long I was in there, and I was advised to pack everything I thought I would need.

For however *long*.

I can't say I was nervous at all, just relieved. I had spoken to all of my family and friends, and I had spent a special time with mam and I told her that if anyone asked about me, and my whereabouts, not to deny that I was in St Pat's. I was not ashamed of it then, and I would never be ashamed of making that decision.

Nobody should ever be!

'I am going in, to help me!' I told mam.

'I am fine with people knowing I am in hospital, getting help.' It was the same at work, I wanted everyone to know what I was doing and they were all so supportive.

In the hospital, nobody cared who I was... that I was Kathleen Chada, who had lost her two boys... whose boys were murdered by their father. I never felt anyone looking at me. Everyone else was in there for their own personal reason.

They were working through their lives. In the dining room, again because of Covid, we were all sitting at individual tables. It was like a school room, basically, it was so unsociable; and yet out in the TV room, strangely, we were all sitting close to one another, and people were able to talk.

My first week, I did not talk to any other patients. I was half-afraid that my psychiatrist was going to give out to me for not talking to the others, but instead she stressed that I was 'in here' for me, and nobody else… just me.

As my room was next door to the TV area, I could lie on my bed and listen to what the others were watching, and that was actually quite nice.

It was a tiny room; a single bed, en suite, wardrobe, no TV. I had Netflix on my phone, and I had books. From the first night, when I lay my head on the pillow with the lights out, I felt I was in a good place.

I had no idea how long I might be there. I had handed myself over to the experts, and I had no fear.

My fear did not enter St Pat's with me, thankfully.

Every day, I spoke with someone.

The psychology side of it all, for me, wasn't brilliant, but that was because I had my own psychologist outside of the hospital and I had a great relationship with him, and trusted in him implicitly. Engaging with the psychologist in the hospital seemed temporary.

There were a couple of nurses in particular, who just knew how to be with me, and what to say, exactly. They were incredible, though at the same time I got to understand how easy it would be to feel hopelessly institutionalised.

There was so much routine.

For the first few nights, until my Covid test results came through, I had been in a small ward, but then I got my little private room. Breakfast was at eight.

I would come back to my room and sleep for another hour or two.

I'd get up and make the bed.

Take a shower.

I only went outside a little bit.

I did a little bingo, though I was not at all fussed about the social side of my time in there.

After that, I'd tidy up a bit.

Have lunch.

Suddenly, it was afternoon, then just as suddenly, dinner. Then bed. I tried to be in my bed by 10 or 11. I'd take a sleeping tablet most nights. Occasionally, one of the nurses would drop in for a little chat, and these late visits triggered some emotions for me. There were nights when I cried. Nights when I actually laughed.

My stay in St Pat's was five weeks, before I came out on a homecare package which lasted for an additional two weeks. I was not nervous about leaving. I was advised that I could go, if I wished, and I was content with that; I realised there was nothing to be gained by me staying any longer.

I also left knowing that if I ever had to return, then it would just be a normal happening in my everyday life.

Do I anticipate having to return there, when my mam dies?

I don't believe I will have to, because I have learned from the experience of dad's death and the manner in which I was dragged to that dark place. But, if I have to go back to the hospital, I will go back in. There is nothing wrong with doing that.

If you cannot get yourself out of *that* place, then there are people, brilliant professionals whose job it is to help you do that. I also know other things.

I am a woman who has suffered an unimaginable trauma, but I am also a woman of 52 years of age, and there are elements in my mid-life, just like everyone else, where there is new 'stuff' going on which can be difficult and disconcerting.

I remember asking the consultant one day… 'Is this all about the loss of Eoghan and Ruairi?

'Or is it also a mid-life crisis?

'Did my loss exacerbate a mid-life crisis?

'Or did a mid-life crisis exacerbate my loss?'

It doesn't really matter which way it is, does it?

I HAD come home from Saudi Arabia, because Sanj wanted me back.

After his travels, he had moved back to London and there was a six months period where we did not see one another. In that period of time, I made my decision.

The rule was that we had to give three months' notice at the hospital in Riyadh and during that period I was not allowed to leave the country. Coming home, for me, was the 'make or break' in our relationship.

I was coming home to try to make a future with him.

In the beginning, I flew to London to have as many long weekends as possible together, but I was living in Dublin and had taken a job here. I was working with Sims IVF Fertility Clinic in Rathgar on the south side of the city.

It was the late summer of 2002.

Over in Saudi I had been worried about where I would get work when I came home? I was working in fertility, and there were only three fertility clinics in Ireland at that time, so I thought the UK was my best bet. I had no idea that experienced fertility nurses were thin on the ground here. Luckily, my mam was listening in to the *Gerry Ryan Show* on radio one morning before I came home, and she heard him interviewing Anna, the manager of the Sims Clinic at the time.

She contacted them, and told them that her daughter was coming back to Ireland from Saudi and was looking for a job. She was told to get me to phone as soon as I was back, but in my head, I was going to London to live. I delayed making the call.

Finally, I did phone and, apart from taking a three years' break in The Kilkenny Clinic (another fertility clinic), I have been working at Sims for the last 20 years.

However, the morning I was interviewed for the job, I was flying out to London as soon as it was done. Mam was driving me to the airport. I was offered a job as soon as the interview finished, but I didn't accept, not straightaway.

They needed me to start the following Wednesday.

I had told Sanj I was offered the job in Sims. He knew that I had also been looking for jobs in clinics in London. On the Tuesday, I flew back to Dublin. But that evening I got a phone call from London to say there was a job now waiting for me there too. *Dublin or London?*

I decided to see what it was like at Sims.

I loved it.

Sanj and I agreed that flying over and back for long weekends was no longer going to work. It was time for him to make his big decision, and he decided he wanted to live in Dublin. Soon, very soon, we were looking at a three-bed semi-detached in Saggart. My family came up from Carlow to look at the house one Sunday and, the same day, Sanj and I placed a deposit on our future home.

We were committing to one another.

Hindsight will tell me that we probably rushed things, but we had been in a relationship for six years at that point, and we knew what it was like to 'live together'. We wanted to live together, formally. We had never owned, or even rented a property as a couple, and we had never experienced a normal day-to-day existence in one another's company, but it felt the right thing to do at that time.

I loved him.

I GOT pregnant a couple of weeks after we put the deposit down on the house. It was very unexpected. I blame Ryanair.

Sanj's flight back to London had been cancelled. We had bought our house off the plans and were waiting for it to be built, so he was still working over there as we sorted out our finances.

Initially, I felt devastated.

What are we going to do now?

We had a year's wait before the house was built, and we had planned to do some travelling together, maybe go back to Saudi for a little bit. It was still the early days in my time at Sims and with the house not ready, and with Sanj delaying before finding work in Ireland, we felt we had options.

Suddenly, we didn't!

I got a pregnancy test kit and took it home. I was living with my younger brother, Ken and his girlfriend, Jean, and when they came in they found me in the floods of tears. They were delighted for me and gave me big hugs, and they left when Sanj arrived into the apartment. He was shocked. But he accepted it after a little while; unlike both of our sets of parents. Those conversations were going to be a whole *other* thing.

Sanj and I sat and discussed our baby.

Nobody was to blame.

We talked and talked that evening, and we decided to get married. We had already discussed getting engaged, though that step in truth was really something we had decided to do in order to keep our parents happy, as we would be living together.

One weekend, we had announced to my parents that we were engaged.

The following weekend, I told mam and dad that I was pregnant. I was on my own; Sanj had gone to London to break the news personally to his parents.

My mistake was telling my mam first, and letting her tell dad, but that was something that she wanted to do. When I met with him, it was one of the first times in my life when I saw him massively upset. He did not say anything to me. There was just silence. I could look into his face. And when I did so, I felt overwhelmed by his disappointment... in me! His girl. I had let him down badly. Deep down, I knew it would be fine, and I knew for sure that he would be a great grandad.

Sanj's parents were the same, simply disappointed. I think, like my parents, they were worried about what people would 'say' and, for instance, my mam had told me that she wanted to tell people, her family, friends. When she did, she discovered that they were all delighted for her and dad. We were 32, but at the same time I was the first amongst all of the cousins in the extended family to get pregnant out of wedlock.

The next day after hearing the news, dad had driven me to the station in Bagenalstown. There was still silence. At the station, before I got out of the car, I leaned over and kissed him, and he did kiss me back, but there were no words. None.

After Eoghan was born, he would tell me and mam that those few days were one of the greatest regrets of his life, and that he felt so disappointed in *himself* that he did not put his arms around me, and hold me and hug me tight.

By then, Billy Murphy and Eoghan Chada absolutely adored one another... which I always knew would be the case!

THEN, AS we went shopping for our engagement rings, something strange happened. We were in the car, and we were arguing.

We were arguing because I would not even consider a termination of my pregnancy.

Sanj brought up the subject.

I'm not sure why, and I don't believe he actually wanted to do anything like that, an actual termination, but his annoyance surfaced once I made it known that there would *not* even be a discussion.

It was bizarre.

He gave me the impression that he did not want the responsibility of a child.

He'd have to settle down, get a real job, be responsible.

Was that it?

I was very upset.

WE DIDN'T buy a ring that day.

I knew what wedding band I wanted, it's called the History of Ireland ring and it's quite a thick band, and I knew I needed to buy that one before we purchased an engagement ring, because my fingers are so short.

We ended up buying the two rings on the same day, a few weeks later.

When I got pregnant with Ruairi, that was also unplanned. And that was when the 'blame' came out in our conversation.

While I was in Saudi Arabia, I had had a laparoscopy, an exploratory surgery. I was having very painful periods, and they had a look at the abdomen to see what exactly was going on with me.

They diagnosed endometriosis.

This is where the lining of the womb, which we shed every month as a period, is growing in places in the abdomen, in the ovaries, or the bowel or bladder; places outside of the uterus. It can cause scarring, and discomfort and pain, and can affect fertility.

As a result of this, I always thought that I might have difficulty having children. We were not taking precautions when I got pregnant with Eoghan, but we did afterwards.

We never discussed having a second child, or not, and I remember saying to Sanj at one point that maybe it will happen and maybe it won't.

But I also told him that if he absolutely did not want another child, then he needed to look after the contraception on his side.

We never actively discussed it over a long period of time.

I was quite happy to have another, but when I got pregnant with Ruairi and I told Sanj, I got the silent treatment from him initially.

My response was that we 'did this' together.

The silence continued for about a week.

This was really shocking at the time, and again, I was really upset with him.

This time, there was no discussion about a termination, but I know he felt that I had purposely got pregnant with Ruairi, and I felt very angry with him.

Thinking me underhanded, and capable of doing such a thing.

I felt isolated.

But I certainly was not going to be the one to break the silence. We were living in Ballinkillen at this stage, having remained in Saggart for just over two years before making the move down to Carlow.

When Eoghan was born we had made the decision that Sanj would become a 'stay at home' dad.

He was dabbling in stocks and shares at this point. He would continue to do that, and I would continue to nurse.

When I came back from maternity leave with Eoghan, I had

been promoted to Nurse Manager, and this came with a pay rise which meant that we could now afford for me to be the primary earner in the house.

We didn't have a car at the time, and we were not going on expensive holidays, so it was a good decision to make.

I look back on that now with regret, of course, and with the realisation that if I had insisted on Sanj getting a full-time job, then maybe things might have been different. He would not have had the time to get further mixed up in his stocks and shares, and gambling.

We were living in Dublin, but we were heading down to Ballinkillen maybe three weekends out of every four. I was working Tuesday to Saturday, and I had Sunday and Monday off.

It was totally natural to spend more time in the country with my parents.

I also wanted Eoghan to go to a small school, in Ballinkillen if possible.

All of us siblings, we had all received a site from mam and dad, so we knew that moving down to Carlow was a real possibility.

We could actually live the dream of building our own home. House prices were going up fast all over the country, and we found that we sold our place in Saggart very quickly once it was placed on the market.

We rented in Leighlinbridge while our house was being built, just two fields away from mam and dad. Sanj and I had spoken at length about the move.

It was easy for me, because I was moving 'home' and had my

new job in The Kilkenny Clinic, but he insisted that he was totally happy with our decision to get out of the city.

He seemed to love life down there.

He liked the idea that Eoghan was growing up in Ballinkillen.

He also made more friends in Carlow than he ever had in Dublin.

EOGHAN WAS born in Holles Street in Dublin... June 26, 2003.

Ruairi was born in St Luke's in Kilkenny. .. February 5, 2008.

With Eoghan, I was doing my antenatal course with a local midwife back home in Carlow. One beautiful morning at the start of my maternity leave I had gone to the beach with my mam, to Blackwater in Wexford, and I got sunburned on my face and my belly. I had big panda eyes, because I had been wearing my sunglasses. At the class, later in the day, I went to the loo and noticed I was bleeding. I came back to the class in shock.

I said nothing for a minute or two, and then started to cry. And I think I scared all of the other mothers-to-be in the class.

I felt terrified. The midwife wanted me to go to Kilkenny, but I felt I needed to be in Holles Street, which was right beside the apartment where we were staying. My mam and my brother picked me up. Kevin drove my car back to mam's house.

It was about 10pm when I phoned Sanj. I was having pains. The bleeding had stopped when I arrived at the hospital, then started again. Sanj was there. They examined me, and brought me into the delivery room where my waters were broken. Things happened very quickly after that.

I had an epidural, and Eoghan was delivered very quickly in the end, but he was immediately taken to the nursery on the ward because his temperature and blood sugar were low. I was so excited to see Eoghan, and was already looking forward to breastfeeding him. However, because of the epidural, I was unable to move.

A little later, I was on my way back from the toilet when a doctor appeared with Eoghan in his arms, and he told me that he was taking him to the special care unit because he was still a little concerned. I wasn't allowed to go with them.

Eventually, when I did see my baby, he looked a bit shocked. He had been about three weeks early, and he was only five and a half pounds; he looked tiny.

Two weeks earlier, I had found out that I was having a boy, though I did not tell Sanj, who didn't want to know. Though he knew that I knew. From the first time he held Eoghan, I could see that Sanj was a natural father.

Ruairi also arrived into this world with some drama attached to his entry. I was working in Kilkenny at that time, so that's why I had him in St Luke's, and Ruairi, like so many Asian babies was also on the small side; he too was five and a half pounds.

I had just gone on maternity leave when I had a routine appointment with my gynaecologist, who did a tracing and an ultrasound. A small anomaly showed up, which concerned him, and so he admitted me overnight before being discharged the next morning. He then planned to bring me in at the end of the week and induce me.

All that seemed fine.

Then they did another trace, and Ruairi's heart rate dropped. In the space of the next hour, his rate dropped three times. There was now some panic. I knew things were serious. I was told they were going to bring me down to the theatre for an emergency section.

I didn't know how serious it was, until I said I wanted to phone my husband, and was immediately told he would not get to the hospital in time. They were moving fast. Sanj was 40 minutes away.

He arrived just in time. We didn't know whether we were having a boy or a girl? Ruairi was just about 35 weeks gestation, and was brought to the Special Care Unit for the first 10 days. I was kept in for a week. One afternoon I walked into the unit and they were doing an ECG on him. They could not get a proper reading because Ruairi's chest was so tiny.

Ruairi had a small hole in his heart, a murmur. He was referred to the Children's Hospital in Crumlin for further tests, but he never looked back, and grew into a strong, healthy little boy.

As with Eoghan, Sanj was the first to hold Ruairi.

Sanj was never an emotional person, apart from when it came to the boys. From the very beginning he was like that, and I remember he found it very difficult when one of the doctors was doing an echo on Ruairi's heart, and was using a probe which he had to push quite hard. Sanj found that difficult to cope with.

He was emotional when Eoghan was born, and extremely emotional the day of that echo on Ruairi. As they grew up, he was also proud of them and their achievements. I think he felt that was *on him*, in a strange way.

He was an extremely hands-on dad, a fun dad.

As I look back on it now, I realise fully that he was there for them at the very beginning and he was the only one with Eoghan and Ruairi at the very end.

He chose himself to be there with them.

I did not get any opportunity to say goodbye to my boys the day they walked out of our house, or hold them after they were killed. At first, I did not feel anything about that, there was no resentment.

But I am resentful now.

He got *time* with the boys.

As part of my Victim Impact Statement I made it clear that he held them for the very last time while they were still warm. I did not get that, Eoghan and Ruairi were cold and still when I got to hold them in my arms.

As a nurse, I have been around dead bodies, and I have been with patients when they have passed. There is an essence about the person in those first few hours, a *presence* still, which fades and disappears as the hours pass.

I always felt blessed to be with a dying patient.

I thought it a privilege.

THERE IS a piece of jewellery I am now aware of, which includes sound waves, with a baby in the womb depicted in lines.

It sounds incredible, and something unique to have forever.

What I have is even better.

I have recordings of the boys voices on a memory 'stick', and this was mainly down to Ruairi who had gone through a phase of recording things on my mobile phone, thinks like… 'Hi, I am Ruairi… I am five!'

There are some of the two boys together.

'Hi, I love my brother… Oe.'

'Hi, I'm Oe… I love my brother Ru.'

I have about 150 of these, and even though most of them have Ruairi simply messing, they are the dearest things to my heart. At the time, after their deaths, I would play them all of the time, though now, I dip into those recordings maybe once a year.

The most important thing is, I know that I have them.

That's so, so important, because it was only after the boys were taken from me, that I realised I had so few photographs of the two of them with *me*. There were an awful lot of photos of Eoghan and Ruairi and their dad, but I always seemed to be missing; taking the same photos, I guess.

Also, I lost so many photographs.

They were *lost* on me, when the Gardaí took away Sanj's laptop, and the PC, and both had all of the files corrupted when they were returned after the court case. Sanj's phone, which had contained so many photos, also seemed to 'disappear'.

I know the computers were held in Garda Headquarters in the Phoenix Park for a long time, and whenever I pass that building, I can't help thinking… *What if I went in, would they maybe find something?*

What did they save… what did they keep?

What did they do with them in the end?

Are they on some disc… somewhere? In the cloud?

I am left with a very limited number of photos.

But this is something that I cannot dwell on, I have to let it go. I know, at the time, my biggest fear was that Sanj would plead some form of diminished responsibility, or plead insanity, so when it came to anything to do with the trial and his conviction, I was… 'Whatever you need to do, whatever you need… take what you need!'

Whatever needed to be done in order to see justice for Eoghan and Ruairi, and whatever was needed to see him locked up behind bars. *Anything.* Anything to stop him being declared insane.

There was a video, where we were all at a friend's wedding, and Ruairi was on the dance floor all evening, whereas we could not get Eoghan out of his seat. I would love to see that video again, just once.

However, I do have my favourite photo that I took of them

that morning, that Friday morning before we had to fly out the door to school. And I have another one.

It was taken by a stranger

We were camping the weekend before the boys were killed.

We didn't camp often, but we had arranged to go to Wexford that weekend. On the Wednesday, Sanj was found to have embezzled money from our local community council.

I was so angry with him, but I was not showing anything in front of the boys. We were able to drive onto the beach, and we were able to erect a tent for a couple of nights.

It's a photograph of us as a family, me and Sanj, and Eoghan and Ruairi, and I had it hanging in my sitting-room in Ballinkillen right until I finally moved from Carlow, and took an apartment in Dublin, in 2022.

I saw it as a reminder that we were a happy family, once upon a time. And that it was okay to remember that we were also a happy couple, once. That's why I had that photo on the wall all of those years. It is still important, to this day, for me to remember that we *were* a happy family. If I try to erase all my memories of Sanj, then I am going to erase so many memories of Eoghan and Ruairi too, because they are intrinsically linked.

Of course, I had to do an awful lot of work in order to allow myself to go there.

But there were happy times with Sanj too. It's important to remember that there were good times. We were happy.

The boys were *happy*.

Their smiles and their laughter, and their playfulness, all of these memories come from within memories of a happy family. The moments of pain, those devastating moments in the lives of my boys, were literally at the very end of their lives, just *moments*, as they awoke in the car and found their dad about to kill them.

Fractional moments, horrific and terrifying which came at the very end of their lives.

They were two boys who were never verbally abused. They did not grow up in difficult circumstances. They never had any reason to be scared, and they were never frightened before that last day.

Eoghan and Ruairi were happy, contented, loved boys.

Normal kids in a loving environment, and in that photograph taken by a stranger of the four of us on a beach in Wexford, we looked a normal, happy family, except of course only Sanj and I knew that the photo was a lie aswell.

The dad in that photograph, that day, had just broken my trust for the first time by stealing from our friends and neighbours in our community.

I DON'T go back to that week… that day.

It is always *there*.

It is part of *me*, that Sunday.

July 29.

2013.

What happened that day shaped, and will continue to shape… *everything*.

I EXAMINE that day, those days that followed, for lots of reasons. As unbelievable and bizarre as it may sound, some of those reasons are positive.

There was the connection with loving people.

My community, and those people, wanting to be there.

Wanting to help.

My family.

Their amazing strength which shone through the greatest horror.

Again, bizarrely, I find it hard to think negatively about those days. What had occurred, and what was happening, was so far *beyond* a word like negative.

There was the pain.

And the grief which I thought would tear me apart.

Tear many of us apart.

There was all of that.

Also, there is the thought that never goes away…

What could I have done to change it?

And what could I have done which might have meant that it couldn't have happened?

But…

I also know there is nothing I could have done.

If it hadn't happened that day, or the night it happened, it would have happened another time.

But... some other time...

Would I have been able to somehow stop it, some other time?

TEN DAYS before, I found out about the embezzlement.

There was a phone call from my mother. 'Kathleen, can you come over?' I assumed it was something or other about dad.

It was a Wednesday and Eoghan had gone off with Sanj for a golf lesson. I couldn't find the keys for the second car, so I phoned Sanj and told him that I had to go over to my mam's, that there was something wrong. He clicked straightaway what it was; I didn't know that at the time, but I found out later that he knew he had been found out.

Sanj had the keys to the second car with him, so I set off across the fields with Ruairi to mam's house. I was walking Ruairi fast, through my brother's field, through the school field, through the graveyard… to mam's, a route I often took.

She was in the middle of getting lunch and, to me, all seemed fine, but I asked her what was wrong and she told me Fr Declan had just been in and that Sanj was after embezzling money from the community centre.

The committee had decided that Fr Declan should inform my mam, to begin with. She was the church sacristan, and poor Fr Declan was the one tasked to make that tough house call. Mam and dad were pillars in the community and the committee was right in making the decision that they should be the first in the family to know what had happened.

I could not understand anything she had just said to me.

Stolen money from the centre?

Sanj?

Mam said she knew nothing more than that.

€56,000.

SIX MONTHS earlier or so, he had gone to the AGM of the community centre with a few of his friends, with a view of some of them being on a committee, and working for funds for a new astro turf pitch.

There was an astro turf not too far away, but locals felt that we should have something like that in Ballinkillen Lorum Community Centre. As he was going out the door, I did joke with him about *not* coming back with a job.

He came home as the club treasurer.

He was a 'stay at home' dad, he had time on his hands to help out. He also had a finance background, so I could see why he agreed to do it, and I could also see why he took it on. The job gave him access to the club's accounts.

I don't know the details of what he did, or how he did it, because I was so angry with him from that evening until the Sunday, 10 days later, when he took the boys. I knew I would find out, eventually.

And then, when the boys were killed, I no longer cared about the money. But that Wednesday when mam told me, I quickly phoned the chairman of the centre and he confirmed what Fr Declan had told my mam.

I also phoned Sanj.

He didn't answer. I left a message. After a time, he answered but throughout that afternoon I still had no idea where he went or what he was doing, as he had asked one of the other fathers to pick up Eoghan after his golf lesson. With Ruairi by my side, I was trying to hold it together. The Gardaí hadn't been told anything. But I knew that they would be informed at some stage, so a couple of days later I had Sanj go to the garda station voluntarily.

Sanj had needed the money for his losses in gambling on stocks and shares, on the US market mainly. He had good money following bad, but I have no idea how he got himself into such debt. We already had some debt on two credit cards, but only a small amount, seven or eight thousand euro; it wasn't tens of thousands we owed.

The sum he took was also not a massive sum, it was *only* €56,000; it was money which might have been got, legally, anywhere. It looked a manageable amount, so why did he do what he did?

I never found out how much he owed to friends. There were, I believe, three or four guys he took money from, in order to 'invest' on their behalf. His cousin and some friends, and one of those he had already paid back.

I thought he was as honest as the day is long but, in hindsight, there was always a side of Sanj that wanted a 'quick fix', and he was lazy. He talked about his trading a lot over the years and in Saudi we had invested some money through a trading desk in Citibank. I put in €2,000 once and he put in more money than that, and we made some money and took back our initial investment, and then he continued. We were never going to lose much money, and I never took it seriously, though I think that he was seduced by the easiness of making that sort of profit.

He then thought he could do the trading himself.

Making money quickly is a gambler's mindset, I guess. When his father had retired and received a lump sum, I know Sanj invested on his behalf.

I didn't understand the seriousness of it all, and it wasn't affecting me, and it never did affect me and the boys until that final week. I feel selfish in saying that but, honestly, I had no reason to dwell on it at all.

Of course, I was deeply embarrassed by what he had done in Ballinkillen. Through that first Wednesday afternoon I spoke with him a few times on the phone and I told him straight, to come home, that we would deal with it all. He came and collected me at mam's, eventually, and we had our first stony conversation about what he had done.

Mam took Ruairi away for a while, and Eoghan was still in his friend's house.

It was just me and Sanj at home. I told him that he needed to tell me everything, and not to leave anything out. When he hadn't come home for those few hours my greatest fear was that he was about to do something to himself.

'Please, do not do something stupid!' I remember telling him, more than once. He went to get a beer, and I was angry, and I told him not to think he could drink the problem away. There was a massive tension there. But all of my thoughts, outside of my anger at him, were about fixing the problem, and I believed we would do that, and as part of that I made him go to our solicitor in Carlow for advice.

After the boys were killed, I was told that we could have solved the issue of the stolen money, that it was 'manageable', that there would have been a court case, but that Sanj in all likelihood would not have gone to jail. We would have ended up somehow paying the money back to the community; we would have turned to my parents, to Sanj's parents, to family to help us find the money.

We had equity on our house; we could have sold up and lived in a caravan behind my parents' home. All of this was going through my mind for those 10 days. We were facing a big problem, and it would be tough, it would be painful, but we would get through it and come out the other side.

I went into 'practical' mode.

I made the phone calls. I contacted Gamblers Anonymous, and sought their advice through their family support. I know Sanj went to at least one meeting in those 10 days, because he came home with a booklet.

As it happened, that summer I had taken parental leave for the first time in my working career, and I was in the middle of five weeks off from Sims which included two weeks of leave. The first week we went over to London to see Sanj's mam. Eoghan's birthday was June 26 and we decided to celebrate him in Sanj's home, and we had a great time. It was his mam's first time to host one of her grandkid's birthdays and she was delighted making that happen.

We drove over, getting the ferry from Rosslare to Fishguard. The boot was packed with presents coming home. I thought we were both in great form, and we even talked about me going back to a three-day week at work, if we could afford it? Sanj would occasionally bring in income, though it was never much. From his trading there was no income, which is why I never took it seriously. I thought it was a pastime. Everything came through my account from my wages.

On that Wednesday night when we found out everything, I remember my mam asking me if we were okay for money? And I told her we were; our mortgage was being paid, our bills were being paid.

We were okay. Luckier than the families of many gamblers.

IN THE subsequent days, after that Wednesday, things remained strained between us. But, at the same time, life had to go on.

Sanj was sleeping in the spare room.

We were due to go camping the next weekend, and everything had been booked and paid for, and I was determined that this was going to happen. The boys were looking forward to the adventure of it all, sleeping on the beach in their tent. They were bringing their bikes. When you have kids it's easy enough to ensure that *life goes on*.

The tent had two separate bedrooms.

Sanj slept with Eoghan the first night, and I slept with Ruairi, and the second night we swapped around. Camping, everyone tucks in at night at the same time. We barbecued on the beach, got a takeaway, and those two days Sanj made a huge effort to give me time and space, taking the boys off as much as possible while I read my books. We moved around a little too, and went to Hook Head where we took the family photo. It was the only time I allowed him to put his arm around me, for that one photograph.

Coming home, I felt stronger still and I was ready, thinking... *Okay, what do we do next?* I was determined to put a plan together to get us out of the whole mess, but one afternoon I also recall Sanj asking me, 'What does this mean for us, as a couple?'

I told him I didn't know.

Because I didn't, and I felt it was going to take a long time as a couple, with counselling, to get through the year ahead of us; the court case, the shame and embarrassment, the nurturing of us as a family, and the recovery of us as a couple. I was not going to kick him out of the house. He was the boys' dad. But, as for our future together as a couple, I was not certain. There was no hiding from that.

Meanwhile, I felt at the same time that he really wanted to put his head in the sand, but that wasn't happening. It was the first time that I viewed him as a weak person. Prior to that I had always thought of him as quite strong and decisive, so witnessing a different him was tough, it was disturbing. It changed my perception of the man I had known for almost 20 years, but, with kids, you mellow, you soften, you are more likely to forgive.

He foolishly thought that he would take the money, win more money and replace the money in the community account, and nobody would be any the wiser. He was adamant, when I asked, that he did not go to the AGM with the intention of taking a position and taking the community's money. He ended up forging signatures, allowing the transfer of money. And he was transferring the money to an account I did not know anything about.

We'd had two accounts. My account, and a joint account. I did not know anything about a third account in his name. He was upset, and stressed, that was clear to me, but I made sure that he talked to his own family about what had happened, and I also wanted him to tell his mam. I gave him a weekend to think it over, and then the following week I told him he had to *tell* her. I know I was doing this for selfish reasons also. If we were going to be asking my parents for some help, then we were also going to ask his mam for help too, on some level.

He put off telling his mother.

The week we came back from our camping, there was a calmness about him, as though he thought the worst was over. I had spoken to him about getting a job. This was now a reality, since Eoghan and Ruairi were both in primary school and my parents were on hand as a support. He hadn't worked for 10 years in a full-time job at this stage.

He needed to get his working life back together. He had family in the UK in business, and if necessary maybe he could start there, making his first few steps in getting a career up and running again.

I genuinely was not worried about the 'calmness'.

I thought it was relief manifesting in him, that everything was now out in the open, and he didn't have the stress of hiding it all from me anymore. But, now, I wonder… I really believe, in truth, though nobody can ever confirm it, was that he had made a decision in his mind as to the outcome for him and the boys.

HE KNEW.

I believe he *knew* what he was about to do.

People have said that there can be calmness about a person who has made the decision to end their own life.

Sanj had made his decision, I believe that.

He knew that he was not going to be around for very much longer to deal with the mess he had made. For him, it no longer mattered.

His focus was on Eoghan and Ruairi.

ON THE Friday evening, I went to an outdoor Mass in Killoughternane, with Ruairi, where there is a Blessed Well. Mam was there before me, so Ruairi got out of my car and went to join her. I was too embarrassed to leave the car, to be honest.

I had the window down. Near me I could her a conversation in another car, and a woman's voice enquired… 'Did you hear about the money going missing?'

I was mortified.

They didn't see me, but when I got home and the boys had gone to bed, I felt incredibly angry with Sanj. I told him how I was feeling, and of the impact his act would have on the boys, and mam and dad. Sanj said he would talk to Eoghan.

I was happy for the two of us to sit down with Eoghan, but Sanj insisted that he would do it. But I also felt a need to talk with Eoghan, and I remember chatting with him about what his dad had done, and I said that he had done something wrong. I tried not to make too much of it; Eoghan was still only 10 years old.

In my mind we had the whole month of August before Eoghan was back in school, and was vulnerable to any of his classmates saying something to him. Also, if a trial was going to happen quickly, Eoghan would have been very sensitive to that. Sanj was his hero.

And Eoghan had a good sense of right from wrong.

At the time, he did not say too much about it to me, there were very few questions, and I guess I was shying away from it too, as I didn't want him to have to process too much.

We have time, I thought.

We have loads of time.

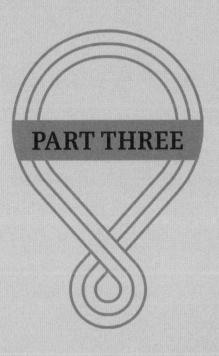

PART THREE

I JUST said a quick 'Bye' to Eoghan and Ruairi.

There were no hugs.

They were going bowling with their dad in Carlow town.

I was going for a walk with my friend Suzanne soon after they were gone.

'Bye… see you later!'

They were my final words.

I probably added to be careful on the road, but I can't remember.

I can't remember either if I was looking at them as they went out the door. Eoghan was wearing his Canterbury tracksuit and his Ferrari baseball cap. Ruairi was wearing a Middlesboro football jersey.

Or, if they had looked at me.

It was 6pm… Sunday evening, maybe closer to 6.30pm.

I get angry now, when I think about it. I get very angry.

I never had the opportunity to say anything else to my boys.

HE TOOK everything.

He literally took… *everything.*

I never got to give Eoghan and Ruairi a last hug.

When they came back to me three days later, they were cold.

WE WERE a huggy family.

And my boys were huggers and cuddlers.

I know there are so many people, like me, who have lost a loved one and wish they had one more chance to say something, one more hug.

A hug that would go on forever.

And when I imagine that final hug, and when I wish that I knew this was the last time I would see them, the questions come…

How could I not have known?

How could I not have suspected anything?

I have done an awful lot of work to try to answer those questions, but I always conclude… *He made sure I didn't know!*

He took everything away from me, right down to those final few moments when the boys were in my company that final time.

He worked so hard to make sure that I didn't know.

Logically, I can understand that, but I was Eoghan and Ruairi's mother and I find it devastating that I didn't know.

They were gone…

As soon as they walked out that door that Sunday evening, they were gone.

Forever.

I believe he was waiting for the opportunity. After the boys were killed, I found an email that he had written, it was a suicide note. In it, it was the whole family he was taking.

It was an email addressed to a friend of his; I have no idea if it was ever sent.

It was written about a year and a half earlier.

I LAY by my husband in bed for all those nights, for well over a year, and I now know that he intended to kill me and our sons, and himself presumably.

The intention had been there for a long time.

The embezzlement was just a tiny trigger. But reading this email, I was forced to retrace my whole life with him, which can be torturous; because you question everything… everything, everything… *everything*.

I found the email about five weeks later, when I was going through Eoghan's emails. Sanj had sent the email from Eoghan's account to his own. He had set an email up in the names of both boys when they were born, so that he could send photos of them over to his family in England.

After Eoghan's birthday in England, I had been onto him to write thank you letters to everybody, but, on the Sunday he took the boys, Sanj had sat down with Eoghan to thank people on email. It took me a while to access the account, because the computers had been taken out of the house. But I wanted to read the emails, and I knew that he would also have had photographs of the boys and I wanted to find them too.

His phone was gone, with photos on it.

The computers were gone, and the digital camera we had bought and which we had used on our camping trip the weekend before, was gone. I needed to find photographs.

And I knew I would find them on the emails.

I was reading the replies to Eoghan's 'thank you emails', and then I went through some old stuff, and I then came across this mail which he had sent to his own account.

At this time, he was in the Central Mental Hospital.

I talked to mam about what I should do with it, and I quickly sent a copy to the hospital and also to the Garda Liaison Officer so that he could forward it to the murder investigation team.

Every night, someone was coming over to stay with me, but it was early evening and I was sitting at home on my own, at the kitchen table, using a laptop my brother-in-law had given me. I was already seeing a psychologist at this time, and I printed out another copy to talk it through with him.

Why didn't he?

Why didn't he take me?

One of our friends who stayed with me for a couple of nights was Eoghan's godfather, Garry, who was a very close friend of Sanj's especially. He asked me if it was okay if he went to see Sanj?

He hadn't been allowed visitors in the early days in the hospital, but this was about two months later. I was happy for Garry to go and see him. I was still in a really strange place when it came to Sanj. I still worried about him, I still cared in some way, and had concerns for him. On another level, I hated every piece of him. It was a really difficult, strange place I was in emotionally, and the fact that someone was going to go and see Sanj offered me some reassurance. Garry asked me did I want anything from Sanj, did I want to ask him anything?

I did.

I wanted to know why he hadn't tried to take me too?

Garry told me that Sanj had been very subdued, and they had barely made eye contact through the whole visit.

He told me that Sanj believed that if he had taken me, it would have been harder for him to do what he did, because he knew that I would have fought him.

After killing our boys, he had made at least two attempts to take his own life, I understand, and each was incredibly pathetic. He had tried to hang himself, and the branch of the tree had broken. I can't understand how, after murdering Eoghan and Ruairi, how he was unable to take his own life.

What stopped him, why didn't he just do it?

Then he drove to a pier, near Westport, and he sat there for a number of hours apparently. He drove around, and stopped to get some petrol. Eoghan and Ruairi, all of this time, were in the boot of the car. They were dead.

The boys were killed around five o'clock in the morning, hours and hours earlier. Initially, it was my understanding that he had strangled them with his hands, but, afterwards, I was informed that he had used a rope. He had been in the back of the car with the boys, and he had constructed some sort of thing with a rope, and the rope was around Eoghan's neck and Ruairi's neck, and his own.

WHEN I had awoken that Sunday morning, I started reading.

He was in the spare room.

I don't know if the boys had noticed the separate bedrooms, but they had never said anything to us. Sanj got up, and he brought me up a cup of coffee, which was not unusual, it was something we did for one another regularly.

In a busy house with two little boys, weekends were calm and we often offered up one morning to one another, and did a little pampering. If I did Saturday morning, he would do Sunday morning.

When he handed me the cup of coffee he mentioned that he was thinking of bringing the boys out later, to go bowling in Carlow town. If I wanted to do something else, he mentioned, then I could; there was no need for me to come with them if I didn't want to.

'Fine,' I told him, but he said that he hadn't said anything to the boys, in case something changed their plans. I was fine with that too.

I got up and out of bed, finally, and we all pottered around through the morning, and at one stage I chatted with Suzanne and we agreed we'd go for a walk later, after Sanj and the boys had gone off bowling.

He made the boys their favourite Indian meal, Dahl and rice. I was always so proud watching the boys eat that, as it was such a healthy plate of food... lentils and veg and good things, and unusual for children to like such a dish. In Indian cuisine, it is usually a side dish. He made the dish for us all.

It was around 2.30pm.

They must not be going bowling, I thought.

Suzanne was coming around to me at 5pm, and just before that he had finally told the boys about his plan for the three of them to go bowling. I needed something or other dropped off to my brother up the road, so it was decided that Eoghan and Ruairi would do that and that Sanj would pick them up at Kevin's house. They headed out the door.

'Bye,' I said.

Suzanne arrived, and briefly spoke with Sanj, though there was an awkwardness about it. We decided to have a cup of coffee before we went out. Sanj came back into the house to pick up the camera. That is the only thing, that whole day, that I can remember being odd. *Strange*, I remember thinking.

But we had often talked about the fact that we had loads of photos of Eoghan, and so few of Ruairi. We didn't have smart phones, and he would have needed the digital camera if he wanted to take shots of the boys bowling.

He headed into Carlow, and went to Tesco where he bought some treats for the boys and bits and pieces. I don't know why he ended up in Mayo.

There is no reason for him to have gone there.

If he was to go somewhere familiar, it would have been south, because we had spent some time down in Cork. I think he simply drove. And the road to Portlaoise was familiar to him, as that is where my sister and brother-in-law live, and it would have been natural for him to initially head in that direction.

I also think he was conflicted, in a way.

He had been waiting for an opportunity, and had taken it by bringing the boys away with him, but I also believe he was trying to delay the action he was about to take, trying to put it off a little longer. That's what I think, and that makes it even harder for me, because he knew what he was about to do was wrong.

I believe he knew what he was planning to do was wrong, and terrible and evil. At a certain level, I believe, he wanted to stop himself, but he couldn't. I think that's why, that morning, he didn't say for sure that he was going to bring the boys bowling; he hadn't said anything in case 'something changed'. This wasn't a moment of insanity, this was thought out, planned out for a long time.

He had decided not to take me with him.

The same as, when we were in Wexford the previous weekend, he didn't decide to drive the car over a cliff with all of us inside.

I CAME back from my walk, and I think I had a bite to eat. I was watching television. It was about 8.30pm, maybe getting closer to 9pm and I realised that we were running out of milk, and I rang Sanj to ask him to pick up some.

There was no answer.

I went upstairs a little later, and I rang him again.

I could immediately hear the vibration of his phone on the bedside locker, but I guessed he had forgotten it. That would not have been unusual; he had an old Nokia phone which he had brought everywhere, but he had just purchased a new phone and he didn't have a protector on it and he was being careful. He would put it in his shirt pocket if he was bringing it with him, unlike the Nokia which he would slip into the back pocket of his pants.

I didn't think anything.

Only, *Shoot, we'll have to go out in the morning first thing to get some milk.*

I THINK he went west straight from Portlaoise.

From what I've been told, he said to the boys that they were going on an adventure, and that I would be joining them later.

They didn't look stressed to anyone who saw them in Carlow.

Why should they, they were going off with their dad, and he was buying them treats. At some point, Eoghan and Ruairi would have fallen asleep.

Before leaving my brother's house, after collecting the boys, he had taken a selfie. Of himself, with Eoghan and Ruairi in the back of the car.

Why?

Why that random act?

I got copies of that photograph.

But I have not kept it.

IT GOT to 10pm.

I was getting a little bit antsy.

Eoghan had camp the next morning.

But it was still the middle of summer, and it was still bright out.

The bowling might have gone on longer than they planned, and he lost track of time and… *Maybe they went to McDonald's?*

He didn't have his phone with him, to phone me, to let me know.

It was much later than planned, when they had finally gone off. If they got to the bowling alley at 7.30pm, played one game, decided to play another… it would suddenly have been 9pm… 9.30pm.

It got to 11pm, and I phoned my brother, and Brian came down to my house.

I couldn't find the key to the second car.

We had two cars, both a Ford Focus. Mine was a newer model because I had most of the driving to do, to work in Dublin.

He's brought both sets of keys with him!?!

Still, I wasn't at all suspicious, of anything. I was just getting a little worried that something had happened to them on the way home.

SO, I'VE no idea how he took the road to Mayo.

They ended up there, on a tiny narrow road. There's the main road coming out of Castlebar, and then there's Ballintubber Abbey. There's a small, winding road off the main road, and then there's this little lane sort of road.

There were two houses only on the little laneway, one house built, one being built.

That is where he killed Eoghan and Ruairi.

At about 5am, I'm told.

The boys must have been asleep for several hours.

BRIAN AND myself headed into Carlow, finally, to look for them.

I brought his phone downstairs.

I left it inside the front door, with a note written beside it.

Ring me as soon as you come in, I've gone looking for you with Brian.

As we were going through Bagenalstown, a car passed us… and I thought, for a split second… *That's them!*

Brian asked if I wanted to turn around?

I said no, that if it was them, then he'd call me when he got my note.

I calculated that it would take 15 minutes for him to get home and find the note, and I waited, counting down the minutes, as we continued on to Carlow.

We got to the Dome in Carlow where they were meant to be bowling.

It was all locked up.

We drove around the town.

There was no sign of the car, anywhere. Going back through Bagenalstown, Brian asked me if I wanted to call into the guards, but I said no.

'Sure why?' And then I added…

'If they're not at home, I'll call them then!'

We turned towards Ballinkillen.

We turned up the road.

Everything in me was willing that I would see the car outside the house. As you travel up the road, there's a certain point that you can see a car outside the house.

Please God…

Please, please… please

Please be there.

There was no car.

We went inside the house, and called the guards.

It was almost 1am.

THE GUARDS in Bagenalstown acted, the minute we called. They showed no hesitation, they reacted very seriously. I had to email them photos of the boys, and of Sanj, and give them details of the car.

I phoned Sanj's brother, Kesh, to see if he had driven up to him in the North?

We ended the call, but he called me back, asking if he should come down to us? Initially, I said no, but then changed my mind. I was thinking that when Sanj finally turned up, he was likely to be taken away by the guards, for his own safety if nothing else.

I also remember thinking that he will need someone on *his* side.

I knew I would have no time for him; all I wanted was to hold Eoghan and Ruairi, and have them home safe.

Kesh came down during the night.

All the time, I was thinking... *He's got the boys with him... He'll be alright!*

I never had any doubt that I would have my boys back.

But I just wanted them back, straightaway. The waiting to see them was becoming agonising. I never, ever thought the boys would come to any harm.

It occurred to me that they might have taken the ferry from

Rosslare to Fishguard, as we had all done a few weeks previously. I suddenly believed that he must be going to England. The passports were still in the house, but, probably, he could get on the ferry with just his driving licence. The ferry would have landed in England about two in the morning. Another few hours to get to his mother's.

For sure, I felt he was gone home to England with the boys. That made *some* sense.

He'd be there by 6am.

Kesh and I waited, and at 7am we phoned their mam.

Suman, their sister, answered.

They had relations from India staying with them for a few days, and Sanj had told me he would wait until they had left and then he would phone his mam and tell her everything about the embezzlement.

Kesh was on the phone to his sister.

She went outside to see if our car was there…if Sanj and the boys were out there, waiting for the house to wake up?

I was leaning against the island in the kitchen. My hands were clenched tight. I wanted to close my eyes, I wanted to pray… *It'll be there… It'll be there!*

And I was wondering… *How am I going to get the boys back from England?*

I will… I will…

Mrs Chada… Suman… they won't let this happen!

I was thinking what flight I could take to London as soon as possible?

There was no car.

I phoned two of our closest friends over in England, but the car hadn't turned up outside their houses either. He must be holed up somewhere, I resolved… frightened.

I knew the boys might now be terrified.

What's Eoghan thinking? Ruairi?

There was a lot of coming and going in the house. Family, friends were waking up to what had been happening through the night. One of my brothers went over to mam and dad's house at about 8am. They arrived in to me.

I went into the bank, to see if there was any activity on our joint account? Nothing. As I left the bank, I could hear helicopters. I didn't know why they were there, I had no idea that they were already doing an initial search of the river. The Barrow. They were looking for the car near the river.

Brian was with me; he knew.

He never said anything to me, thankfully. I had been awake all night, and everything was a little fuzzy. A detective came out to the house from Carlow, and he wanted to know if it was okay to interview me immediately?

We went into the sunroom, it was 3pm… 3.30pm by now.

The phone went.

A lot of phone calls had been coming through, but this number popped up on my phone that I did not recognise. The interview had started. The detective was starting right at the beginning… Where I was born? Where I was raised? Where I went to school? I didn't know it at the time, but he was trying to paint a picture for himself of my life… our lives.

We were halfway through this, when that strange number showed up on my phone.

It was him.

I was thinking stupidly, I guess. I had watched so many detective shows, and I was thinking... *They'll want me to keep him on the line for as long as I can!*

'Sanj, are you okay?' I asked.

He told me no, and said something about crashing the car, an accident or something, it all sounded muddled to me. I asked him about the boys?

Eoghan?

Ruairi?

'No... they're dead in the back!'

No...

They're dead...

In the back.

No...

They're dead...

In the back.

No...

They're dead...

In the back.

I screamed. I think I screamed. I vaguely remember screaming.

I HAD no idea to the degree of harm he inflicted on my boys.

It was only much later, around the time of the trial, that I found out how much Eoghan in particular had suffered.

Learning what I did, of what he did to Eoghan and Ruairi, I can never stop thinking how anyone can ever believe Sanj Chada has served enough time to justify his freedom. He did not *just* kill Eoghan and Ruairi.

There is a difference between killing somebody, and what he did and how he brutalised them. But I was told very little at the beginning, and it was explained to me why this was so by the Garda Liaison Officer who was so kind and supportive. He explained why he could only share portions of information but, that later, at the trial, if there was to be a trial, that I would find out everything I wished to know in advance.

If he pleaded any kind of defence, there would be a trial. I would be called as a witness. Knowing this possibility, I was adamant in those early days that I did not want to compromise anything, I did not want any technicalities to work in his favour at a trial. There was, at this stage too, a part of me thinking that he must be insane.

He had to be insane, to do what he did?

How could he not be?

As time went on, I realised he was never insane.

Our undertaker, Edmond Kearney is a family friend, and he and his wife and family have become a huge support in my life. They have done so much for me. It was Edmond who assured me that if there was ever anything I needed to know, that he would be there for me. He promised.

I didn't want any pussy-footing around. My boys had been murdered, my life had been destroyed. I wanted to know everything. And, Edmond has seen so much in his working life. He knew how to tell me, and when the time came he was gentle and totally honest with me.

I had been thinking that if Sanj had died, or if he was to die, I would bury him with our boys, but Edmond also told me he would not have let that happen.

'You wouldn't have been able to stop me!' I told him.

He told me it would not have happened.

He would never have allowed that to *happen* to me.

It was not easy for him, but he also spoke with my brothers. To have such a strong, kind person watching my back all that time, when I knew so little and was so confused and conflicted, is something for which I will forever be thankful.

EOGHAN HAD a fist of his beautiful hair pulled from his scalp.

His collarbone was broken.

His arm had been damaged, and his hip.

He suffered extensive head injuries.

The official cause of Eoghan's death was strangulation.

Eoghan had fought.

My little boy must have fought with everything he had.

Edmund Carney had a lot of work to do in restoring Eoghan's skull, as he prepared him for me and his family.

Sanj says that Ruairi slept through this fight.

I don't believe him.

He says that when Ruairi awoke he placed him on his knee to comfort him, and then strangled him.

I'm left never knowing for sure.

Why would he do that to Eoghan?

Was it all self-hate?

Why would he have been that angry?

I know that I can never sit in front of him and ask him.

I pray that Eoghan lost consciousness as quickly as possible.

And I pray that Ruairi did not see everything.

EVERYONE IN the house knew what I heard on the phone.

I had come back out of the sunroom and into the sitting-room, and sat down on the couch. Everyone was sitting and standing, waiting.

Someone said, 'No, they can't be dead'.

I could hear voices. I was thinking…

He crashed the car… He's able to ring me on a phone…

They have to be stunned…

Unconscious.

They can't be dead.

The detective who had been interviewing me said he had to go outside to make a call, and he'd be right back. I didn't know that he was about to get confirmation that Eoghan and Ruairi were actually dead.

I stayed sitting, in front of the window in the sitting-room. A minute or two later, he walked back into the room.

He looked at me.

'I'm so sorry Kathleen… I am so sorry!'

I often think of how hard that must have been for him – knowing he was about to change my life forever.

THE TRIAL was due in October.

A Tuesday.

On the Saturday before that two detectives came to us, and sat the whole family down and prepared us for what we were going to hear. But I already knew some of it.

We had already been informed that he was pleading guilty.

But we all knew that until he was asked the question, and until we heard the word 'Guilty' from his own mouth we could not be certain.

HE HAD phoned from the crash. He was still in the car.

He had borrowed a phone from somebody.

Nobody on the scene knew what was going on, and they didn't know my boys were in the boot of the car.

He had crashed on purpose.

He had heard the CRI Alert. A Child Rescue Ireland Alert had been issued about 2pm and details of the car were up on signs on motorways. I would later be told that this was the first CRI Alert in the country. Thankfully, every case since has had a successful ending.

On the radio, he also had heard that the Gardaí were looking for his car. He had been parked up somewhere, on a side road in Westport, and then made the decision to drive at speed out onto the main road and into a wall.

A few days after the funeral, I went down to Mayo and met with the guards. I went to where the boys were killed and I also went to Westport, where the crash had happened. Looking at the road he crossed, he could have smashed into someone walking, or a cyclist, he could have killed somebody else. This was another attempt to take his own life. He had so much time if he really wanted to kill himself, eight or 10 hours. He had more than enough time; I have no knowledge of his true intention.

There was hardly a scratch on him when he was found. Only his collarbone was broken. When people came across the crash he still had a rope around his neck, and the car was locked. They had to break the side window to get to him. The air bag had been deployed. He had hit the kerb on a footpath before hitting the wall.

He had been trying to harm himself, still, when someone finally got to him.

He asked for a phone. He was reaching out to me. Or perhaps it was just instinct. I'll never know why he finally called me.

He was brought to Castlebar Hospital.

Eoghan and Ruairi were also brought to the hospital morgue.

When I was told there was a need to identify the boys, I wanted to immediately go there, but the detective stopped me. 'Kathleen, maybe it's better if it's not you who goes,' he told me, and in my state of shock, I understood and agreed.

Brian and Kevin, my brothers, set off with two guards.

When they left, my sister, Irene brought me upstairs. We went into the boys' room, and I lay down on their bed and Irene lay behind me, and she wrapped her arms around me and held me tightly through the night.

I fell asleep for a little while. I was exhausted, but I knew I needed to start thinking straight. I don't know how or why, but I felt a need to be aware, to be capable, to take in hand whatever was about to happen next.

I woke up when I heard a car coming in. It was the dead of

night, it was Brian and Kevin back home. The house was still full of family and friends, some asleep in beds, others lying on couches. I came downstairs.

I understood that this was my last chance… *There was a mistake!*
It wasn't Eoghan and Ruairi.
It wasn't them.

I could see that Brian and Kevin were distraught. I knew then. One of my cousins described the sound I made that second as the sound of my heart breaking – she was right.

'Did they look okay?' I asked.

They assured me that someone would be staying with the boys through the night, that they would not be alone in the morgue.

They told me that the lights in the morgue were going to be left on all night.

I wanted to go and see them… I wanted to hold them, but I didn't ask anyone to bring me to Castlebar. I was still in a deep state of shock, and disbelief, I guess. I didn't know at the time how badly damaged Eoghan had looked, so perhaps there was someone looking down on me, guiding me… *Gran Murphy?*

Sanj was nearby in the hospital and if I had gone down, I would have asked to see him, and that would have been a mistake. In my general state, I may have shown him too much attention, and care, and I am so glad that I was not there at all. It might not have lasted long, but any care at all would have left me with a massive regret.

If I had seen him, and if we had shared even a brief moment of grieving together for Eoghan and Ruairi…

I hated what he had done, but I don't believe I fully hated my husband at that point.

I was in a vulnerable state. I had needed Gran Murphy's guidance, and for the second time in that 24 hours she did not fail me.

Kesh was with us, and Sanj's mother and sister came over on the Tuesday, and a neighbour brought her over to Castlebar to see him in hospital, but he refused her. But I think he would have seen me.

I NEEDED to get Eoghan and Ruairi home.

The post-mortem had been carried out, but for legal reasons there was a delay in their bodies being released. Behind the scenes, there was a discussion I was not aware of, of bringing me to Castlebar.

It would have been to say my goodbye to my boys.

I was later informed that I would not have been able to touch them, just view them, and if that had happened it would have been too hard.

Edmond Kearney and his father, Tom, were worried that any further delay might prevent them from having the boys back at home to wake them in open coffins. They feared that I might never get to touch my boys, or kiss them.

On Wednesday evening they were told that they could collect Eoghan and Ruairi. I watched as the evening news on RTÉ showed the hearse leaving the morgue.

Edmund had kindly placed the boys together, in the one coffin. He would tell me that, passing through one town, there had been a festival on and he had been asked if he was carrying Eoghan and Ruairi. When he said that he was, the celebration stopped in the town and a guard of honour was immediately formed. He told me it was an incredible, moving tribute from complete strangers.

It was 4am on Thursday morning.

We all drove the seven kilometres to the funeral home.

But I did not see Eoghan and Ruairi there. They were already in the hearse.

I went home behind the hearse.

I had their bed ready.

I had put on new sheets, and their favourite farmyard duvet.

Eoghan and Ruairi were back in the big bed that they had decided to share at the beginning of the year.

My boys were home, and I had them with me for a last 24 hours.

I wished for 48 hours, and asked.

But as a nurse, I was also aware that sometimes bodies do not do well after several days, and I said that I didn't want my boys to suffer any indignity. I knew that an extensive autopsy had been performed on both bodies, and that embalming was going to be a difficulty. I understood why the funeral had to be on the Friday morning.

24 hours…

NO AMOUNT of time was going to be enough time.

And 24 hours was too short.

And 48 hours was not long enough.

I had thought that I would be able to sleep in the bed, between Eoghan and Ruairi, but I could not do it. The boys were so cold, and they were so stiff.

It was not possible.

I placed a mattress on the floor, and slept a little there.

Everyone had left the room.

This was my time with my boys. I did not go into a deep sleep. I was in my pyjamas, and I had a duvet over me. Every few minutes, it seemed, I would wake up and I would get up and watch them.

I sat on the end of their bed.

I lay down beside them for a time.

I went down to the kitchen and made myself a cup of coffee and brought it back up to their room.

I lay down on the mattress… and I sat up again. Several times,

I did not speak to them, there was nothing I needed to say. They already knew that I loved them with all my heart.

I kissed them… and kissed them.

THEY WERE both dressed in their Kilkenny gear.

Eoghan and Ruairi loved the Kilkenny hurling team.

They were peacefully at rest in their bed in black and amber. They looked so beautiful, and they were surrounded by their little cousins, and friends. We were in the bathroom next door at one stage and Lily, who was six or seven at the time, was with her mother. Lily was really worried that Eoghan and Ruairi, in their beautiful Kilkenny jerseys, were going to 'get all dirty' when they were put into the ground.

My nieces and nephews brought them presents, and sweets, and left them on the bottom of their bed, and one of them left a toothbrush. She had told her mummy that Eoghan and Ruairi would still have to brush their teeth in Heaven.

Emily reached out to take one of the sweets.

'No, no,' her mother said, 'Eoghan is bringing them to Heaven with him.'

'Sure Eoghan wouldn't mind, mammy,' Emily replied.

And that would have been true.

Sarah, who was the same age as Ruairi, there was only six days between them, was sitting on the bed watching the movie *Tangled* on her mam's phone. The two of them had always been as thick as thieves. She had sat down beside Ruairi.

She was wriggling into him, as if to say, 'Will you move over!'… and then she got fed up and went around to Eoghan's side of the bed and sat in beside him instead.

Eoghan, I know, would have been happy to watch the movie with Sarah, but she would have had no hope whatsoever of getting Ruairi to be still or pay attention.

I LOOKED at them, and I knew my boys were at peace.

For everything that they had gone through in those horrific last few months, they had still found peace. I could see that clearly.

All of the children who were in and out of the room all through that Thursday morning and afternoon, and into the evening, could feel that peace too.

So many good and kind people came, and bravely paid their respects, and I know that it wasn't easy for any of them.

The goodness of people was extraordinary.

The Kilkenny manager Brian Cody came into the house with Henry Shefflin.

I had to break it to Henry that he was not 'King Henry' in our house… that title belonged to 'King Tommy'.

Tommy Walsh had been in the local school grounds training the kids once, and Ruairi had managed to get a ball past him.

Tommy turned up later that night.

THERE WERE some smiles.

We wanted to celebrate the lives of Eoghan and Ruairi, and that was vitally important to me too.

One of my cousins, Anne Moloney, landed into the house and she had a bag of stuff with her. She was coming from Ennis, and she was trying to think what I would need, so Anne went shopping.

She bought black, black and... *black*.

Anne and I spent plenty of time together growing up, along with lots of my cousins. And I had lived with her for a while in Navan. We still laugh about the fact that she might have secretly hated me as a kid.

I was the oldest and only girl in my family for 10 years, so I was spoiled silly. Anne was the youngest in her family. She arrived with milk and bread, toilet paper, and sanitary towels, Anne wondered did I have black tights?

A black dress?

When she arrived, we hugged. There was no need for any words.

We went upstairs to my bedroom and she started dipping into her bag of clothes. The dress was put on a hanger and hung up at the front of my wardrobe.

I remember talking to her after, but she doesn't really remember – she just needed to do *something*, just like so many people did.

In truth, she was being practical, and she was minding me. She was in shock the same as everyone but that did not stop her going into overdrive. Funny, she says she cannot remember buying anything.

I didn't actually wear Anne's dress.

I already had a black dress, which I wore with a red cardigan.

We all did a lot of smiling.

I believe, because of the level of devastation within the house, and the darkness which had enveloped it, there had to be a release in order to… survive it all, and get through those days. Even if it is only momentarily escaping the dark, dark place.

I was in the middle of it all.

Some people, who did not know me, arrived to pay their respects to other family members, and I remember directing one couple over to Irene and Donal, who then immediately returned to me with the same two people.

Nobody expected me to be visible.

But I was determined not to be drugged up, or hidden under a duvet.

I needed to be present.

In my family, we all come from a very practical background, and that is what got me through that first week. I think logically. I live in a world of grey, but often my head is black and white, and I knew very quickly what I needed to do to get through those days.

I was not going to get my boys back.

This was my last opportunity to celebrate Eoghan and Ruairi with my family and friends, and there were just five days to do that before their funeral. If I was not present for those five days, I knew I would live with regret. From Monday to Friday, I had been very adamant in my own mind… *I need to be making decisions. I need to be present.*

I can fall apart next week.

I ASKED my parents, and Sanj's mam, to say their goodbyes to Eoghan and Ruairi while they were still in their bed. I just wanted their uncles and aunts present as they were placed in their coffins.

Liam, Kenneth, Kevin, Brian and Irene were in the bedroom, with Sanj's brother, Kesh and his sister, Suman.

As I dressed, I remember thinking that I wanted my boys to be proud of me, of how I looked and how I held myself. We were walking to the church, so I remember thinking… *Comfortable shoes.* The things that go through your mind can be quite odd. On the Wednesday, waiting for the boys to come home, I had been walking down the stairs and I immediately asked Anne to do some dusting. All I could see was this layer of dust. I wanted the house right.

It is surprising how you can notice so much. Inconsequential things become important.

When we were leaving the house the hearses were one in front of the other, but when we turned up the road towards the church they were driven side by side.

I was also surprised by a song.

Twinkle, Twinkle Little Star

As we were leaving the house, my nieces and nephews began singing… walking beside their parents, amongst themselves they decided they wanted to sing something. They were only toddlers, babies… but they were amazing.

As we approached the church, I could sense crowds of people. After that, I don't remember everything as clearly.

I was cocooned.

I didn't see people, or faces.

But I was still thinking of him.

Having lost my boys, having lost everything that was precious to me, he was the one I wanted to lean on. Even though he caused all of *this*. It took a long time for me to hate him. I loved him. He was my husband, and my partner for almost 20 years and I had loved him for so long. He was Eoghan and Ruairi's father.

I kept telling myself to put him to one side, to forget about him and anything he was going through. I kept reminding myself to think of the boys, *only*.

The two people I found it most difficult to be with through those days were my mother and Sanj's mother. I think that's because of the link from our children, to a mother, to their grandmothers? There was the strongest connection between them and Eoghan and Ruairi, the same as there was that brilliant connection between me and Gran Murphy.

I could feel their pain more than anyone else's… I physically felt their pain, and at the same time I was trying to manage my own pain. It was so hard to hold them close.

With mam, I could talk things through and manage, but with

Mrs Chada, when she hugged me, tightly… I felt she was never going to let me go, and I *needed* my space.

Mrs Chada was obviously devastated, and in a way that was different to everyone else. He was her boy. She needed to hug me. But my state of shock and emotion was almost *physical*, and it was almost like my nerve endings were tingling when some people touched me.

By Friday morning, I could not understand what was wrong with me?

My cheeks were so sore.

But, I realised, because I am only five feet and two inches tall, everyone was pulling me into them for a hug, and were holding me tight, and then holding me that bit longer, and I was hitting my cheeks against the shoulder bone of most people. I was bruised on my cheek bones… the strangest feeling.

THERE WERE no words spoken between myself and Mrs Chada.

None that I can recall.

There were no words to say.

After me, she was the next person in the most pain.

Her shock must have been the equal of mine.

Her boy.

Her son.

He had done this.

The Chada family stayed with very good friends of mine, Carmel and Paddy. I know it must have been hard for them, but knowing his family were with such good friends eased my mind.

I don't know why, but I needed my house to be *mine*. For me and my family.

That might have been hard on them, too, but I could not share my house.

AS THE boys were being lowered into the ground, I started to panic. Suddenly, I was consumed by a fear that Eoghan and Ruairi had never been anointed.

There were so many priests on the altar, a total of 16 I was later told, and Fr Declan and Fr Pearse were two I have been very close to, as they would have been to my house many times. I was thinking… *It's too late.*

I must have been saying this aloud, because someone overheard.

Fr Charlie McDonnell, the parish priest in Westport, had been on the altar. I did not know him at that stage, though he has become a dear friend since, who helps me, and offers me his home to stay in when I travel west. He had been called to the crash scene.

Fr Charlie was quickly by my side, at the graveside, and he assured me that they did not need to be anointed, and that they were going straight to Heaven.

'I did confirm them,' he also told me.

'I didn't think they were old enough to have been confirmed… I hope that is okay?'

That gave me an immediate sense of *rightness.*

It offered me immediate comfort, and even though I am not

overly religious as a person, to know that they were going straight to God, to Heaven... it made sense to me.

A calmness washed over me at that moment.

I transformed from a ball of tension and stress at the grave, to an almost beautiful calm. Everyone had been invited back to The Railway Bar in Bagenalstown after the funeral; it was Eoghan and Ruairi's favourite spot, and they adored the lamb shanks there. Frankie Doyle and his son, Mark had ordered in lamb shanks for all our family and friends, which was more remarkable kindness of thought.

The sun was shining as we left the cemetery.

It was a lovely summer's day.

SEPTEMBER WAS awful.

The boys should have been going back to school.

It was a date and time that had not been looming over me, actually I had forgotten all about it, and that was the problem as it turned out. I was driving up the road to my mam's house this one morning and I passed the school, and saw all of the cars and all of the kids. First day back! I had not thought about it, or imagined it, and I felt a double blow to my solar plexus.

It was a blow to me, but I also felt for the children going into the school. I do know that they had psychologists in the school for the first few days, and they were also in the local secondary schools in Bagenalstown and Borris, for the children who would have known Eoghan and were now starting first year there.

The Monday that Eoghan was killed, a birthday present had arrived at the house for him. It was from my brother in Australia, and his wife and children. It was a poster of hurling sticks, and it was presented in the Ballinkillen colours which are just like the Tipperary colours... blue and gold.

I subsequently had it framed, and a local artist, Siobhán, brilliantly inscribed the boys' names on it, and it now sits on a wall in the national school alongside a photograph of the boys.

DID I feel I was going mad?

I had no suicidal thoughts in that first year, which may appear strange, but I had started seeing a psychologist very early on, within the first five weeks. And that guided me. I would sit with him three times each week. I honestly feel that meeting him made all the difference in me keeping my sanity.

I never had those thoughts, but there were many occasions when I wished that I was not here. I would think, for instance, that if I was diagnosed with a cancer that I would keep silent, and not seek treatment, and allow nature to take its course. I was not going to take my own life, but if it was being taken from me at that time, I would have let that happen. I don't feel like that anymore.

My 'out of control' feelings and thoughts were trying to understand *him*?

The man who murdered our boys.

It was, I believe, about a year and a half before I started living fully with my grief. It was much easier to concentrate on him.

What he had done?

Why he had done it… how he had done it?

The person I thought he was, versus the person I discovered him to *be*.

Everything was about him.

There was only one moment, that I can recall, that I felt an impulse to ring him. I was sitting in my car, and I wanted to talk with him. So, I got out of my car and had a cup of tea… and composed myself. I resolved that if the need remained, then I would make the call.

I never needed to again.

There were a couple of sessions with my psychologist where I would hold a photo of *him*, and I would speak with him directly that way. It allowed me to say things, express myself, but it was never going to give me any direct answers.

I never asked *him* why, because I am afraid of the answer I might receive. I know there are no answers to this, that no answer could ever be okay. If I had to listen to him justify what he had done, in any way, I feared it might push me over the edge.

All I know is… *he* had it in *him* to do this.

He had it in him because he is an incredibly weak man, who is egotistical and narcissistic, and selfish… though those words, any words I might choose, are inadequate to describe the man he is.

How could you do it?

How could you have this inside of you?

I had to stop asking why… and I finally did. I understand that I will never actually need any answer. Any answer might touch upon some form of justification.

There is no justification.

There is nothing he can ever say!

Some of his friends had visited him, and they always checked in with me first to make sure I was okay with them doing so, but in time he withdrew from them. He stopped taking their calls, and stopped writing to them.

I imagine every time he was in contact with them, he was being confronted by what he had done. If he did not have to speak with them, then he was not being challenged.

As far as I know, the only person he now has contact with outside of Arbour Hill Prison is his mother; he calls her once a month. It's a six-minute phone call each time.

It was an awful lot less painful for me to concentrate on him, far less painful than thinking about Eoghan and Ruairi. For the first 18 months they lived somewhere in my consciousness. Logically, I knew they were dead, but it took a long time for me to believe... *They are dead, and they are not coming back.*

There was this vague, unreal notion somewhere in my head that they might come back. The full acceptance that they would never come back took a long time after that, and it was the most painful time of all.

In the early days, nearly all of my time with my psychologist was about *him*.

How could I not have known?

How did I lay next to him all that time? How did I love him?

Why didn't I go with them?

Could I have handled things? Changed things?

At one sitting, I remember saying to my psychologist that surely I needed to take some responsibility? Not for what he did, but... I needed to take responsibility for the relationship I had with *him*.

A relationship in which he couldn't talk with me? A relationship in which he could hide things away from me?

It took a long time to navigate those questions.

To understand…

Sanj did what he did, *himself*.

He is a bright, articulate, intelligent man.

He knew what he was doing, and he killed our boys for his own selfish motives. Because he could not face the person he had become… the gambling addict, the liar, the thief.

He did not want the boys to see him as that man.

The man he really was!

They adored their father, and he did not want to destroy that.

He had been found out.

The boys were going to know.

And in that year and a half, too, I had to question everyone else around me. *Who can I now trust?* If I was so wrong in trusting this man, whom I had loved for 20 years, and had two children with… *who could I trust?*

A SOCIAL worker in the Central Mental Hospital made contact with me, and told me that Sanj was asking for some things from our house.

I agreed.

The day after the funeral, I had gone into 'My husband is in hospital mode' and, bizarrely, I packed a bag of clothes to be sent up to him in Dublin. My brother-in-law, Donal and my dad said they would bring the bag up to the hospital.

I had a shirt and tie in the bag.

I remember holding the shirt and thinking there will be a court appearance coming up soon, and he will need this shirt and tie. I could have brought the bag up myself, but I was scared of my own emotions. I was afraid of asking to see him, and then being allowed to see him, and feeling sympathy for him.

What would that do to me?

I was terrified of opening up that door.

The social worker said he was asking for some books.

He was asking for a photo of Eoghan and Ruairi.

And he was asking for a photo of me and him.

I sent them off.

She asked if he could write to me?

Initially, I said yes. But I also told her that he should know that I would not be responding to any letter.

One letter came, and two more after that, before I said I did not want him writing anymore. I was in the kitchen on my own, when the first letter dropped in the letterbox.

I was trembling, but I opened it straightaway. It was in an envelope, within an envelope, and I recognised his handwriting which was very distinctive.

A one-page letter.

It told me nothing. He was just writing it for selfish reasons. There was not even an apology. I had thought that there might be some insight… *something*.

As a couple, we had our moments, but we were never a romantic pair. I was looking for something in the letters; clarity, insight, *anything*… instead the letters bordered on love letters. He quoted lyrics from songs and he talked about the boys and, it seemed, unbelievably… as though he was trying on some level… to comfort me?

This was within the first two months of Eoghan and Ruairi being murdered. They came within a three weeks' period, first one, then two the same week.

How Long Will I Love You was in the charts at the time.

It was a song I loved, and it was a song I shared with the boys. It was *ours*.

How long will I love you?
As long as the stars are above you…

The letters were hopeless. Worse, they were infuriating.

I said enough.

The only insight I had, perhaps, came from letters he had written in the car in Westport before he crashed into the wall. I did not have access to them until after the trial date.

There was a letter to his brother.

Another to me.

One to Eoghan and Ruairi.

He called Eoghan a 'magician'. He called Ruairi a 'treasure'.

To a certain extent, they were just rambling thoughts from someone who had just taken the lives of his own sons. When they were read out in court, one of the lines absolutely devastated me. It was in the letter he had written to Eoghan and Ruairi and he had claimed...

'Mummy is getting rid of me....'

I was sitting there in the courtroom, when I first heard this... *He is blaming me!*

I FIRST saw him in the courthouse in Castlebar, when he was handed the book of evidence. It was about six weeks later, and I was surrounded by my family.

It was a regular day in court in Mayo, and totally surreal, with defendants present to answer charges of not having insurance, or a tax disc being out of date. License extensions. Or small-time drug dealing.

We drove from home. We got there early and met the detectives who, as always, were so good and so kind. They allowed us in early to take our seats, before the courtroom was actually opened to the general public. We sat at the back.

He was brought from the hospital in Dublin.

I felt terrified.

Seeing him, and what emotions would surface upon seeing him. Though we realised very quickly that the judge wished to have his case heard quickly, and get it over with. But, there was no sign of him.

At first, I thought he had killed himself.

He's killed himself in the back of the prison van.

I thought they were going to usher me out, and break the news to me and tell me that he was gone… *He's dead.*

A little part of me was hoping that this would happen.

However, it transpired that the prison staff who were driving him had got lost and were simply late getting to the courthouse. The judge was very unhappy with them, that was plain to see. We had been sitting there for about an hour, listening to all of the other cases. Then, there was a commotion behind us at the entrance.

I saw the side of his head as he was ushered into the courtroom.

He was in handcuffs.

His hair was very long and loose, hiding his face, and all I could focus on was a bald patch on the back of his head. He had always said that when he started losing his hair, he would cut it.

He was just in, and out. He did not speak.

He got up and walked out, and he never looked up.

We were about to head home too, when Brian asked me if I wanted to visit Ballintubber Abbey again?

Going to visit where he had killed Eoghan and Ruairi seemed right at that moment. We arrived, and we were in the gift shop there, and when one of the ladies there realised who we were, she asked if we'd be okay meeting Fr Frank Fahey?

We waited, and he came down to us and we chatted for about half an hour, 45 minutes. We talked about where the boys were killed, and how I had been there the week after that. I told him that I never sensed 'evil there' in that place, when I visited the first time.

He told me he had been up there, at that *place*, too, and that he had prayed there.

Fr Fahey telling me this made sense.

Why would there be any evil around Eoghan and Ruairi, and where they were murdered? There would not be! The evil lived on… *he* did not die there.

Sanj is the evil one. Not my boys. Ballintubber has become a very special place for me. The people there embraced my boys. And Fr Fahey's words of support over the years have been incredible. He has a very special way.

THERE WAS a letter sent to me about the inquest.

Luckily, my Garda Liaison Officer heard about it and alerted me.

I was back at work, and when I got home it was there.

It included the cause of death…

'Ligature Strangulation.'

It was the first time I had been told exactly how Eoghan and Ruairi had died. I had assumed it was by his hands.

There had been no phone call in advance of this letter.

No warning.

To see it written down on paper was so hard.

THE SECOND time I saw him was the day of the case in the Dublin Central Criminal court.

He pleaded guilty.

I DO believe that one day, he will be released.

My greatest fear is that he might turn up in Ballinkillen one day to visit the boys' grave. I believe he does not have a right to do that.

But I believe it might happen too.

I am informed that he is a model prisoner, having adapted well to prison life. None of that surprises me.

I know he thrives on routine. And he has no responsibilities, and lives in a safe environment.

He is amongst his own kind.

I cannot let his possible future release from prison dictate my life.

I have strived to be indifferent to *him*.

But, in reality, I know I cannot be indifferent.

I cannot walk away.

I cannot go to the other side of the world, to Australia… and try to live my life anew without *him*.

I cannot leave it behind. It will always be there.

All I can do is to fight to keep him in prison for as long as possible.

I believe he will be in prison for 23 years… 25 years at best, and the latter part of that sentence might be in an open prison. He is not causing problems in prison, and the average life sentence in Ireland, prior to parole, is 20 years.

I have to stay, and I have to fight.

I have to fight to make changes to the parole law in this country, and to the justice system. But this is a fight I will lose, ultimately. The loss will be when he walks out of the front gate of Arbour Hill. Then, I will have lost.

But I will step up every single time he applies for parole. And he has applied once already, after serving his first seven years. He will apply again in two years' time.

I did not expect him to apply the first time.

That did shock me.

I was informed by the Prison Service, and immediately I had to go into fight mode. Though I am not sure at all how much influence a letter from me actually has on the Parole Board. This is what I wrote the first time…

Parole Application for Sanjeev Chada 1st September 2020

To whom it may concern,

That I actually have to write this letter is an insult to the memory of my sons Eoghan and Ruairi Chada. Eoghan and Ruairi were and are the most precious and loved of boys. They were loving, caring, kind children who loved their lives, their families and each other unconditionally. That love was betrayed in the most brutal way on the 29th of July 2013, by their own father. Someone they loved and trusted totally. What he was capable of doing to them is beyond my comprehension. And should be beyond the comprehension of any human being in my opinion. That he feels entitled after just 7 years to apply for parole, having carried out such a calculated, gruesome act on two innocent and defenceless children for his own gratification shows how inhuman he actually is.

The reasons that he should not be granted parole or any other concessions, having served just 7 years of TWO life sentences, should be obvious to anyone who looks at what he has done. That he chooses to apply in the first place shows the weak and pathetic man he is, with no insight into the ongoing impact of his actions. That impact reaches beyond just myself. It impacts my family, extended family, friends, community and beyond.

How does someone like him be rehabilitated into society? You cannot, therefore he will always be a threat to me, to my family and to society in general.

Regards,
Kathleen Chada

Let's say we get to 23 years, is a new letter from me going to stop him from being released? I will engage with the Parole Board at that time. I will also go to the media.

But, what happens if I just can't do this anymore?

When I have written four or five times already and I might not have the energy anymore? And that is the year he gets out of prison?

That's my fear.

I can never stop fighting.

'JOY' IS a word which means different things to me now.

My nephews and nieces bring me joy, that is true. Though, I realise that I will never be in a position to say that I truly feel joyful about my life, or that I can experience true happiness.

That does not mean that I cannot share joy and happiness with other people and their lives. And I never feel guilty about doing that. But I will always, first and foremost, live my life with loss.

In March of this year, in 2023, I bought a new apartment in Dublin. The day I walked through the front door, I cried.

And the sense of loneliness I felt at that exact moment was crushing. People have said to me it must be exciting, a new chapter in my life which should be great, and fantastic… and it was all of those things, too.

However, I never anticipated the emotion that swept over me as I walked through that door and the realisation that… *I should not be here! I should be in Ballinkillen… with my own family.*

In my own home.

I also knew, if I was walking into a new home… I would be showing Eoghan and Ruairi their new bedrooms. But I will strive to be happy, I know I deserve that. And I know that Eoghan and Ruairi would want that for me… *always.*

Epilogue

IN MY work as a fertility nurse, many years ago, I informally counselled many patients. I saw up close the sense of loss and the pain in some women, and men too. And I saw how they handled their emotions.

Some were consumed by these different emotions. Anger and sadness. And I often wondered how did they present themselves to their family, and their friends and work colleagues?

That experience helped in a small way, in the manner in which I began to process the loss of Eoghan and Ruairi, and how I wished my life to be going forward.

So many different emotions are valid to every one of us.

But, sometimes, our extreme emotions can also alienate us.

As I've said, when I looked at my young nieces and nephews, I realised that if I was Auntie Kathleen, who was bitter and miserable and angry all the time, the kids would not have wanted to be around me. Why would they want to? And I'd lose!

In their lives, I would just be a sad person in the corner of the room. They might be told to hug me or talk to me, but they would have no interest in going out for something to eat with me or go to the cinema together.

They would continue with their happy lives.

I would be left behind, and rightly so.

And it is the same with my family and friends. Their lives must go on at full pace, and be packed with fun and happiness. As I told my sister, Irene, when she has a bad day with her kids it is perfectly okay to give out to me about them.

People are afraid they might hurt me with their choice of words but, in reality, I cannot be hurt any more than I already have been hurt.

It's not that I can't be hurt again. I can.

It's not that I can't feel emotion. I can.

But I can never be seriously damaged as a woman ever again.

•••●•••

I CANNOT remember the last time I was at Eoghan and Ruairi's grave.

From the bedroom window of my mam's house, I can actually see the grave. But that is not where my boys are; and when I go over there and stand by the graveside I feel only frustration, because I am only looking at a slab and a piece of ground.

It is not where they are.

Their bodies were placed in that new grave, and my dad's

body was placed in there too, years later, but I feel no need to be there. To talk to them. To feel them. I know there are people who experience great comfort in visiting the graves of their loved ones, but I do not.

In the beginning I went, because I believed I was expected to go, but that soon stopped while I was still living in Ballinkillen.

I stayed in Ballinkillen for eight years after they were killed, and I thought that when I moved to Dublin, maybe I would go back more often to the graveyard. But, no.

Eoghan and Ruairi were buried side by side.

My dad's body was placed on top of Eoghan's, and when my mam passes her body will be placed on top of Ruairi.

In truth, I sense Eoghan and Ruairi everywhere.

Eoghan and Ruairi are not in that parcel of ground.

•••●•••

I MOVED to Dublin in November of 2021.

I had been comfortable continuing to live in our house in Ballinkillen. But the 'relationship' with that house was conditioned by everything that happened in the eight years I spent there after their deaths.

In the early days, as family and friends rallied, they would not let me have a night on my own. During the days, people were coming to see me all of the time. Neither did I have any desire to go anywhere. They had a rota, too.

It must have been difficult for my siblings, because they had their own families and lives to live, so I used to go and stay with them as often as possible. I would arrive and sleep over, and then go back to my own house the next morning.

At the time, I was unsure if I needed that level of support, but then again, my daily life was something of a blur, I was in such a state of shock for so long.

So, I made the decision quite early on, that I was not going to be tied to my own house. It was not going to become a shrine to my boys. It was their home, and it remained my home, but it was not *everything*.

I knew all the time, that I had to be able to leave it… for a night, for a holiday. Wherever I went, I was going to be bringing Eoghan and Ruairi with me. And I did not leave them when I sold my house in Ballinkillen a year and a half ago.

It had reached the point where I had no comfort there anymore, only frustration. Part of that was because it was such a big house, one that had been built for a whole family.

To me, it needed a family.

The heart had left the house. It was simply walls and furniture. I was resenting having to spend so much time cleaning it, and it was getting dusty as it wasn't lived in. I was just using the living room, my bedroom and the bathroom.

I quickly enough made the decision to sell.

I think I always knew that I would, and when I walked out the front door for the last time it was not an issue for me at all. Though I was a hoarder, and I blame my mother for that.

•••●•••

I HAD to buy a large skip.

It was hard going into the boys' bedrooms and making decisions on their things. I had to make decisions; I could not bring everything with me.

Dropping my wedding dress in the skip had been easy.

But Eoghan had made a robot from cardboard and toilet rolls, and it had sat on his shelf from the moment it was made a couple of years before he died.

It was about two feet high.

Am I going to go with this?

I looked at it, and dusted it off a bit and thought… *If I keep this, I am keeping everything.*

And I can't keep everything.

Someone suggested taking a photograph of it, but if I was going to photo it, then that meant I should keep it.

I said, no.

It's got to go and… it's okay that it is going.

I don't need to do anything special with it. I don't need to bury it, or burn it.

It's just going, and that's okay.

If Eoghan and Ruairi had remained alive, the robot would have been long gone anyhow, because Eoghan was not going to be holding onto it at 20 years of age.

Either he or I would have thrown it out.

It went into the skip.

After that, everything else was easier. There was no need for any drama, things just needed to go because my future home simply did not have enough room for all our stuff. I had loads of offers to help me fill the skip.

But I knew it was something I wished to do myself.

I ended up getting two skips.

Everything was potentially special, and I did not want endless questions of, 'Kathleen, where do you want me to put this?' And, 'Kathleen, what shall I do with this?' I did not want any of that questioning.

My brother came along with his tractor and trailer and pushed everything down tight, so the two skips did the job for me.

•••●•••

THE NEXT stage of my life was moving into an apartment in Dublin.

It was a new me, and it was very different for me. For such a long time, it seemed like my life was defined by the loss of Eoghan and Ruairi. I remain a mother, but I do not have my children with me any longer.

There are many mothers out there who have lost children, and some who have lost more than one child. It's the circumstances that are different for all of us, but the loss is the same. And my loss of Eoghan and Ruairi is the same as any of their losses.

As for me moving on, I had just turned 50 years of age.

The start of a whole new chapter in my life.

The possibility of having any more children was gone. It was probably gone long before this, but it is now really gone in my mind. I am on my own.

And that was a big thing for me.

Bigger than I had ever anticipated, or ever thought. I had had a conversation with my psychologist very early on, that because of the nature of my profession, I knew that I had options if I wished to have a child.

I was turning 43, and needed to consider those options.

I did consider them.

Do I want to have more children?

Do I want to consider fertility treatment with a donor sperm?

I gave myself a year to make that decision, until I turned 44, but midway through the year I knew that it was not something I wished to do. I absolutely adored being a mother. And I would happily have had more children, but I made the decision that I was not going to have a child just for the sake of having a child.

I did not want to be a single mam.

•••●•••

FROM EARLY on, I made the decision to hold onto the name 'Chada'.

My boys, Eoghan and Ruairi were born Chada, so I will always hold onto that surname because of them.

I will remain Kathleen Chada until the day I die.

It is nothing to do with Sanjeev Chada.

The Chada name is on their gravestone, and it remains with all of the special memories that so many people have of my two boys.

The name is my link to them. I was always very proud of holding that name from the time of my marriage. It is a different name.

And it is me now.

•••●•••

I KNEW I wanted to get a tattoo at some point.

And the one I chose is an infinity symbol. You see one at the top of each section in this book, and I carry an infinity symbol on the inside of my left forearm.

It is a continuous line, from start to finish… and one that goes on and on. The symbol on my arm also includes the shortened names Eoghan and Ruairi had for one another.

Eoghan was 'Oe'.

Ruairi was 'Ru'.

It's funny, because when I was deciding on the names of the boys, I was adamant that I did not want names that could be shortened. I wanted Irish names, and I particularly love the name Padraig. But I could not call Eoghan 'Padraig', because everyone would have jumped to call him Paddy… and the first culprits would have been my own family!

'Paddy Chada' was not going to work.

I thought up the name Eoghan, believing it could never be shortened. The same with the name Ruairi. However, when Eoghan was beginning to talk as a toddler he could not get his tongue around his own name… and his best effort was 'Oe'. It stuck in our house.

We kept the fada off Ruairi's name, because the Indian and English side of the family would never have been able to get their heads around that, we thought. We read *Winnie the Pooh* to Eoghan quite a bit, and in that book there is a Roo.

We decided that Ruairi should instead be 'Ru'.

Those shortened names are there on my arm, and also a white feather.

White feathers are a sign of a loved one nearby. However, I did not see any at all in my first year after the boys died. In the next two years, I was falling over them.

The spine of the feather on my arm is part of the circle itself, as the two circles form the figure eight. I got it while I was in Australia visiting my brother, Liam and his wife, Sharon down there about five years ago.

The tattoo artist came up with the idea.

I had no fixed idea what I wanted, but he guided me, and it is there now and it is permanent, and it is not in anyone's face.

I had driven by the shop, in the small town in which they live, many times. Timeless Tattoos, it stated over the front door. I knew the time was right, I had waited long enough.

It is quite big, but I don't care.

It is just for me.

And I can turn my arm over and see it. It's not for anyone else.

It's mine. For me and my boys.